James Donovan

The Keys to Offensive Intelligence: Techniques and Strategies to Collect Information Effectively

Observe, Analyze, and Persuade: Secrets of an Intelligence Expert, Former Special Forces Operator, and Ex-Spy

Horizon Press

Horizon Press – All rights reserved
August 2023

"The real power of intelligence lies in the ability to gather relevant information and turn it into decisive knowledge."

John C. Maxwell

Foreword

James Donovan's journey is an epic narrative defined by resilience, unwavering dedication, and an unyielding quest for purpose. Originating from modest academic beginnings, he embarked on a bold trajectory into the military world, driven by an insatiable desire to push the boundaries of his inherent capabilities. What commenced as a leap into the uncharted realms swiftly metamorphosed into an all-encompassing passion that would intricately shape the very course of his life.

Upon immersing himself in the sphere of military service, James found himself irresistibly drawn to the electrifying vibrancy of the armed forces and the meticulous precision inherent in military operations. His relentless commitment empowered him to confront the myriad challenges posed by arduous training, a process that honed his skillset with each new endeavor. It was through fostering camaraderie, embracing discipline, and cultivating an innate sense of duty that he discovered a profound purpose propelling him through the triumphs and tribulations that punctuated his journey.

Following four years of dedicated military service, James seamlessly transitioned into a specialized role within an esteemed regiment of elite special forces. This pivotal juncture heralded a seminal phase in his life, positioning him squarely at the forefront of military operations. It was here that his innate talents were brought to the fore, as he unearthed a remarkable capacity to adeptly navigate the constantly shifting dynamics inherent in this complex domain. This innate dynamism propelled him into the heart of audacious missions, igniting a fervent passion destined to guide his path for years to come.

In the year 2010, calamity struck as James fell victim to the harrowing blast of an IED during a critical mission. The ensuing physical and emotional wounds would push the limits of his resilience and determination in unprecedented ways. Yet, true to his nature, adversity served to fortify his spirit. During the course of his arduous three-month hospitalization, his unwavering resolve garnered the attention of two discerning recruitment agents representing an intelligence agency. Recognizing his extraordinary attributes, they extended an invitation that would forever reshape the trajectory of his life.

The transformation from the frontlines to the realm of intelligence did not transpire without challenges, yet James embraced this transition with characteristic tenacity. His role as an analyst offered new dimensions of understanding, where information emerged as a potent tool to sculpt outcomes. His tireless pursuit of knowledge led him from dissecting questions related to the Pushto-speaking regions to evolving into an invaluable advisor at the pinnacle of the agency's echelons.

In 2013, an unforeseen opportunity beckoned James back to the field, this time assuming an undercover identity. His two-year odyssey across the African continent immersed him in the intricate tapestry of field intelligence, offering a profound immersion into diverse cultures and challenges that further broadened his perspective. With every mission, he deepened his comprehension of the delicate equilibrium between information gathering and safeguarding lives.

By 2015, James found himself on South American soil, contributing his expertise to a Minister of Defense in a new context. This experience exposed him to the nuances of international affairs and diplomacy, expanding his horizons beyond the confines of intelligence analysis. Returning to the heart of danger in 2018, he ventured into the perilous world of Mexican cartels, extracting pivotal information while operating under the veil of secrecy.

However, as 2020 approached, a catastrophic plane crash above the Iraqi-Syrian region shattered his physical being. This turning point compelled him to confront his own mortality and reevaluate his priorities. With the unwavering support of his devoted wife, Cindy, and the boundless love of their two children, James discovered solace and a renewed purpose in the embrace of his family.

James Donovan's extraordinary odyssey encapsulates the potency of resilience, adaptability, and an unceasing quest for purpose. From the battlefields of military operations to the intricate web of intelligence analysis, he traversed continents and challenges, emerging as a beacon of inspiration. His life story testifies to the indomitable strength of the human spirit, a reminder that even in the face of adversity, the pursuit of knowledge, integrity, and love can reshape destinies.

In the year 2023, a significant juncture in James Donovan's journey arrived as he made the resolute decision to publish his inaugural work, aimed at the avid enthusiasts of intelligence and espionage. This pivotal choice was a natural progression for a man whose life had been punctuated by relentless dedication, profound experiences, and an unquenchable thirst for knowledge.

Drawing upon his multifaceted background spanning military operations, intelligence analysis, and international diplomacy, James embarked on the endeavor of sharing his accumulated wisdom with a broader audience. The culmination of his years spent on the frontlines and within the hidden corridors of intelligence agencies was about to take the form of a literary masterpiece—a profound testament to his enduring commitment to his craft.

James Donovan's unique perspective infuses his writing with an unparalleled depth, merging real-world experiences with astute insights that transcend the traditional boundaries of espionage literature. His determination to provide readers with an authentic and unfiltered portrayal of the world of intelligence shines through as he peels back the layers of intrigue, revealing the nuances that define this complex landscape.

In this forthcoming book, readers can expect to be transported into the heart of espionage, gaining access to the mind of a man who has navigated the intricate realm of classified information, covert operations, and the fine line between protection and subterfuge. James's narrative weaves together personal anecdotes, expert analyses, and gripping tales from the field, creating a compelling tapestry that captures the essence of the espionage world like never before.

As he pens each word with the same meticulous precision that marked his military and intelligence career, James Donovan invites readers to embark on a journey of enlightenment. Whether readers are novices intrigued by the clandestine world of espionage or seasoned experts seeking fresh insights, this book promises to deliver a comprehensive exploration that transcends clichés and reveals the profound impact of intelligence work on global affairs.

"James Donovan: Unveiling the Shadows" is not merely a book; it's an intimate revelation, an invitation to grasp the complexities of a field that often operates in the shadows. By sharing his narrative, Donovan underscores the enduring value of intelligence work and its indispensable role in shaping the world we inhabit. Through his book, he endeavors to ignite curiosity, foster understanding, and inspire a new generation of passionate individuals ready to engage with the captivating world of intelligence and espionage.

In an era characterized by rapidly evolving technological landscapes and ever-shifting geopolitical dynamics, James Donovan's decision to share his unique insights couldn't be more timely. His book is poised to become a cornerstone for those seeking to unravel the enigmatic world of intelligence, offering a nuanced understanding that transcends sensationalism and embraces the authentic essence of the field.

Publisher's Note: Ethics, Respect, and Responsibility

Dear Reader,

As we present to you this exceptional volume delving into the captivating world of intelligence and espionage, we wish to convey a critical message regarding the core values of respect, ethics, and responsibility that underpin any exploration of these subjects.

The realm of intelligence is shrouded in secrecy and mystery, conjuring images of covert operations and intricate strategies. However, it is imperative to remember that the knowledge and skills gained from these pages must be wielded with discernment, ethics, and a profound understanding of the ethical and legal implications.

Espionage and intelligence play a vital role in national security, the preservation of human rights, and global stability. Yet, their improper use can lead to devastating consequences. We implore our readers to maintain an unwavering commitment to integrity and responsibility in all endeavors related to the acquisition and utilization of information.

As you absorb the teachings of this volume, keep in mind the importance of adhering to laws, regulations, and ethical standards. The application of these insights to infringe upon the rights of others, compromise security, or breach legal boundaries can cause irreparable harm and carry severe legal repercussions.

Indeed, this book stands as a valuable resource meant to educate and inform, but it is your responsibility to apply it appropriately and ethically. The methods and strategies shared within these pages should be employed for the common good, security, and protection of the democratic and humanitarian values we hold dear.

The editorial team and authors of this volume stand united in their belief that knowledge should be a force for good. We encourage you to utilize this information to contribute to society, promote peace, and ensure security. We hope this volume sparks enlightened discussions and deep reflections on the role of ethics and responsibility in the complex world of intelligence.

Be mindful of the power of the knowledge you acquire and use it for the betterment of all. Your commitment to integrity and ethics will help shape a better and safer future for generations to come.

With our respectful regards,

Introduction

In a world in perpetual motion, where security, geopolitical and economic issues are intertwined, the art of offensive intelligence is proving to be a powerful weapon for decoding mysteries and making informed decisions.

This book, intended for all those who wish to explore the secret horizons of intelligence, is an invitation to enter the captivating world of offensive intelligence. From the pen of a mysterious author, whose identity remains hidden for obvious reasons, will reveal the keys and techniques that make it possible to navigate the murky waters of information and knowledge.

Whether you are a private investigator looking for clues to solve complex puzzles, a police officer eager to master advanced investigation methods, an economic intelligence consultant looking for strategic levers, or a simple curious citizen, this book will open the doors to valuable knowledge.

Offensive intelligence, far from being reserved for small circles of the secret service, can be used ethically and responsibly by anyone who wants to arm themselves with crucial information to make informed decisions and protect legitimate interests.

By turning the pages of this book, you will be introduced to a range of investigative techniques, information gathering methods, and analytical approaches, while learning to handle the tools of persuasion and communication with finesse.

Captivating stories of field missions, tinged with fact and fiction, will take you on thrilling adventures, where ingenuity, perseverance and foresight play a vital role.

Beyond the fascination of intrigues, this book is intended to be a practical guide, anchored in reality, which offers a clear and accessible vision of the world of offensive intelligence. Each chapter is designed to provide valuable lessons, illustrated by concrete examples and case studies.

Never forget that knowledge is a powerful weapon, and it must be handled with care and responsibility. The offensive intelligence techniques presented in these pages are intended to be used in an ethical and legal framework, in accordance with applicable laws and regulations.

Whether you are prepared to face the mysteries of espionage or simply eager to familiarize yourself with intelligence strategies and approaches, this book will guide you with wisdom and discernment.

Venture into this complex universe where secrecy mingles with light, and discover the keys that will allow you to decipher the enigmas of the world, armed with offensive intelligence.

Ethical issues

At the heart of intelligence practices, privacy is a fundamental principle that should never be neglected. As journalists, private investigators, consultants or ordinary citizens, our mission is to explore the mysteries of intelligence, while ensuring respect for individual rights and freedoms. Every investigation, every gathering of information must be conducted in accordance with the laws and ethical values that underpin our profession.

In this quest for truth, transparency and consent play a key role. Individuals and businesses engaged in intelligence practices must ensure that they clearly inform individuals about the collection and use of their data. Respect for ethical principles is the foundation on which a responsible and balanced investigation rests.

Beyond the curiosity that drives us, it is essential to scrupulously comply with the laws in force. Industrial espionage, hacking or any other illegal practice must be categorically banned from your investigations. The responsibility of each intelligence actor is engaged in the choice of methods that respect rights and ethical values.

In this quest for crucial information, sharing with third parties must be done with caution. The confidentiality of sources and the preservation of sensitive data are ethical imperatives. The information obtained must not be used in a malicious manner or to prejudice the rights and interests of the persons concerned.

The purpose of intelligence must always be rooted in a desire to serve the common good. Each piece of information obtained must be analyzed with objectivity and discernment, in accordance with the values on which our profession is based. By embarking on this ethical path, we help build trust with our readers, while demonstrating our commitment to responsible intelligence practice.

Disclaimer: The author of this book wishes to emphasize that the intelligence techniques and principles presented here are intended to be used in an ethical, legal and responsible framework. Any use that is malicious, illegal or in violation of the rights of individuals is strongly condemned. Readers are encouraged to learn about their country's intelligence laws and regulations and to act in accordance with the ethical standards that guide our approach.

In conclusion, intelligence and intelligence are powerful tools, but they must be handled wisely and responsibly. Journalists, private investigators, police officers, business intelligence consultants and every citizen have a responsibility to comply with ethical values and applicable laws. Exploring the mysteries of intelligence invites us to be actors committed to the preservation of individual rights and freedoms.

Together, let us take up the challenge of ethical information, respectful of the rules and at the service of the common good.

HUMINT Techniques

Beyond machines, sophisticated algorithms and digital tools, lies an essential part of intelligence: HUMINT, or human intelligence. Throughout history, societies have understood that the power to collect and analyze information held by individuals is essential to make informed decisions, predict future events, and protect the interests of nations and peoples.

Human intelligence has its roots in the deep history of humanity. From the earliest civilizations, individuals understood the vital importance of acquiring information about their neighbors, rivals or enemies. Before the advent of modern technologies, human intelligence was the primary means of gathering intelligence.

In ancient times, the Egyptian, Greek and Roman empires already used secret agents to obtain strategic information. Spies were sent to distant lands to gather information about the intentions of their enemies and gather political, military and economic intelligence.

In the Middle Ages, feudal lords and kings employed emissaries to infiltrate foreign courts and report information about the shenanigans of their rivals. These secret agents, often disguised as travelers or merchants, gathered valuable information by listening to conversations, observing behaviors, and establishing discreet relationships with local informants.

The Renaissance marked a period of intensification of human-sourced intelligence with the emergence of black cabinets and special intelligence services in some royal courts. These secret services were responsible for monitoring the activities of nobles and courtiers to prevent plots and betrayals.

With the advent of the great colonial powers, HUMINT played a crucial role in the exploration and expansion of empires. Secret agents were deployed to unknown lands to gather geographical, cultural, and political information, while serving as intermediaries between explorers and local populations.

Over the following centuries, human intelligence continued to evolve with political, social, and technological upheavals. During the World Wars, spies were at the heart of intelligence operations, playing a vital role in gathering information about enemy movements and military strategies.

With the rise of the Cold War, intelligence has experienced an unprecedented intensification, with secret agents operating clandestinely in foreign countries to gather information on nuclear programs, political intentions, and espionage activities.

Today, despite the rise of digital technologies and sophisticated intelligence methods, physical intelligence remains an essential pillar of information gathering. Human agents continue to play a vital role in intelligence operations, gathering sensitive information and establishing trusted human contacts.

Thus, HUMINT, the ancestral legacy of human espionage, continues to evolve, adapting its methods to contemporary issues while preserving the crucial importance of communication and human interaction in intelligence gathering.

Human intelligence is often considered an art, relies on communication and human interaction, implementing skills such as empathy, persuasion and understanding the behaviors and motivations of individuals. This discipline goes far beyond the simple exchange of information and requires the establishment of relationships of trust, the subtle reading of non-verbal signals and the ability to adapt to unpredictable situations.

In this chapter, we dive into the fascinating world of HUMINT. Captivating stories, elaborate methods and teachings from decades of experience will guide you through the mysteries of this ancient discipline. Whether you're a private investigator looking to solve complex puzzles, an intelligence officer working for a state, or a private citizen eager to better understand the world around them, this chapter will offer you a comprehensive overview of HUMINT's techniques.

Each section of this chapter will take you to a new dimension of human intelligence. You will learn how HUMINT practitioners make close connections with their sources, build networks of informants, and collect crucial data that is not in digital databases.

Human intelligence is not free from ethical challenges and dilemmas. Throughout these pages, we will also address issues of privacy, ethical manipulation and accountability in the collection of sensitive information.

It is essential to understand that HUMINT must be practiced in accordance with laws and ethical values. The techniques presented in this chapter are intended to be used in a manner that is lawful, responsible and respectful of individual rights. HUMINT should never be misused for malicious or unethical purposes.

We invite each reader to approach this knowledge with a keen awareness of the ethical implications. The quest for information must never obscure respect for human dignity and fundamental rights. HUMINT is a powerful tool that, when used wisely, can help preserve peace, security and justice.

1. Direct Questioning: Face-to-face interviews to obtain information directly from human sources.

Introduction to direct querying

Direct interrogation is an essential technique of HUMINT, or human intelligence, which relies on face-to-face interviews to obtain information directly from human sources. Since time immemorial, this ancient method has been used to collect crucial intelligence in a variety of contexts, such as criminal investigations, military intelligence operations, market research, diplomatic negotiations, and many other areas where the collection of reliable human information is of utmost importance.

A. Definition and importance of direct interrogation in HUMINT

Direct interrogation consists of face-to-face meetings between an intelligence officer and a human source to gather key information. Unlike digital or automated methods, this approach emphasizes direct communication and human interaction, allowing the agent to detect nonverbal cues, facial expressions, and behavioral cues that can reveal additional information.

The importance of direct interrogation lies in its ability to provide data that cannot be obtained by other means. Human sources can share sensitive information, contextual details, motivations, and emotions that are critical to informing decision-makers' decisions and actions. This technique also helps to understand individuals' perceptions and attitudes, which are not always easily accessible by other methods of information gathering.

B. Objectives of the face-to-face interview

The objectives of the face-to-face interview may vary depending on the specific context of the intelligence operation or investigation. Some of the main objectives include:

Collection of crucial information: The main objective is to obtain crucial and verifiable information from reliable sources to feed the knowledge base of decision-makers.

Data verification and validation: Direct querying verifies and validates information already collected through other means, such as open source or digital sources.

Understanding intentions and motivations: By interacting directly with the source, the intelligence officer can gain a thorough understanding of its intentions, motivations, and perceptions, providing essential context for analysis.

Disinformation detection: Direct interrogation also detects attempts at disinformation or manipulation by the source, helping to assess the reliability of the information provided.

Building trusting relationships: When the agent establishes a relationship of trust with the source, it can pave the way for future information and ongoing collaboration.

Interview preparation and planning

A successful face-to-face interview in HUMINT relies heavily on careful preparation and thoughtful planning. This crucial step allows the intelligence officer to prepare to interact with the source effectively and strategically, maximizing the chances of obtaining relevant and reliable information. In this chapter, we will explore in detail the key steps involved in preparing and planning a face-to-face interview.

A. Identify interview objectives

Before embarking on an interview, it is essential to clearly define the objectives of the interview. What specific information does the intelligence officer want to obtain? What topics or questions are relevant to the ongoing investigation or operation? By clearly defining the objectives of the interview, the agent can focus on the key information needed to make informed decisions.

B. Select potential sources

The selection of potential sources is a crucial step in preparation. The intelligence officer must identify the individuals who are likely to hold the information sought. They may be witnesses, experts, suspects or any other person with relevant knowledge of the events or subjects in question. Preliminary collection of information on these potential sources is also necessary to better understand their background, affiliations and credibility.

C. Collect preliminary source information

Before the interview, it is crucial to gather preliminary information about the source. This stage of gathering information can be done from open sources, databases, preliminary investigations or other reliable sources. This preliminary information will help the officer get to know the source better before the interview, make it easier to prepare a report, and ask relevant questions.

D. Building trust and cooperation

Building trust and cooperation is crucial to the success of the interview. The intelligence officer must take an empathetic and respectful approach to the source. He must present himself in a professional and reassuring manner, clearly explaining the objectives of the interview and ensuring the confidentiality of the information provided.

E. Anticipate possible scenarios and emotional responses:

Thorough preparation also involves anticipating possible scenarios and emotional responses from the source. Some information can evoke strong emotions in the source, such as fear, anger or anxiety. The intelligence officer must be prepared to deal with these emotional reactions with calm and empathy, while continuing to maintain the established climate of trust.

F. Plan interview logistics:

Finally, the intelligence officer must plan the logistics of the interview. This includes selecting a safe and confidential location for the interview, choosing an appropriate date and time, and considering any other relevant logistical considerations.

Interpersonal skills and effective communication

At the heart of direct questioning in HUMINT are interpersonal skills and effective communication. These essential qualities allow the intelligence officer to establish trusting relationships with human sources, thus promoting a fruitful and honest exchange of information. Active listening, reformulation and other communication techniques play a key role in deeply understanding the source's statements and gathering relevant information. By avoiding the pitfalls of manipulation and pressure, the officer preserves the integrity of the interrogation process, while creating an environment conducive to respectful and ethical collaboration. With these skills, the intelligence officer is better prepared to conduct successful interviews and acquire information critical to intelligence operations.

A. Active listening and reformulation

One of the most important interpersonal skills for conducting a successful face-to-face interview is active listening. Active listening is about paying total and focused attention to what the source is saying, being open and receptive to its words. This involves focusing not only on the words spoken, but also on the underlying emotions, facial expressions, and nonverbal cues.

To develop active listening, the intelligence officer must avoid frequent interruptions and external distractions. He can also use reformulation techniques to show the source that he understands and values what it expresses. Reformulation consists of repeating the information synthetically and presenting it to the source in the form of questions or summaries. This practice demonstrates to the source that the agent is attentive and eager to understand his statements accurately.

B. Techniques to encourage the source to disclose information

In a face-to-face interview, it is essential to create an environment of trust that encourages the source to disclose relevant and reliable information. To do this, the intelligence officer can use several techniques:

Empathy: The agent must empathize with the source and show that they understand and respect their feelings and experiences.

Ask open-ended questions: Rather than asking questions that call for a simple "yes" or "no" answer, the agent can use open-ended questions that encourage the source to give more detailed and elaborate answers.

Information validation: When the source shares information, the agent can validate it by showing that they take what is being said seriously and asking additional questions to delve deeper into certain topics.

Respect the rhythm of the source: Some sources may be reluctant or hesitant to disclose sensitive information. The agent must respect their rhythm and avoid pushing them too quickly to share delicate details.

C. Avoid the pitfalls of handling and pressure

Avoiding the pitfalls of manipulation and pressure is of crucial importance when conducting a face-to-face interview in HUMINT. These practices not only compromise the integrity of the interrogation process, but they can also undermine the credibility of the information gathered and jeopardize the security of the source. To maintain high ethical standards and ensure the reliability of the information collected, the intelligence officer must be aware of potential pitfalls and take a respectful and ethical approach throughout the interview.

Do not mislead: The agent must never deceive or lie to the source to obtain information. Manipulation of facts or deliberate presentation of false information can distort the perception of the source and call into question the credibility of the agent and the entire intelligence process. A relationship of trust must be established on an honest and transparent basis to ensure that the information obtained is truthful and useful.

Avoid coercive tactics: The use of coercive tactics, such as intimidation, threats, or undue pressure, is unethical for HUMINT. Forcing the source to disclose information or placing it in an uncomfortable position can not only undermine its integrity, but also hinder the interrogation process. Rather, the agent should foster an environment of trust and cooperation, where the source feels comfortable sharing information voluntarily.

Respect source limits: Each source has its own limits on the information it is willing to disclose. The intelligence officer must recognize these limitations and not push the source beyond what it is willing to share. Forcing the source to disclose information they wish to keep confidential can not only be detrimental to the relationship of trust, but also lead to inaccurate or unnecessary results.

Listen to and consider signs of discomfort: The officer must be attentive to signals of discomfort emitted by the source during the interview. These signals may include expressions of nervousness, changes in body language, or hesitation in responses. If the source seems uncomfortable or reluctant to talk about certain topics, the officer should be sensitive and respectful, avoiding forcing discussion on these sensitive topics.

Creating an enabling environment for the exchange of information

To ensure the success of a face-to-face interview in HUMINT, creating an environment conducive to the exchange of information is of paramount importance. This environment fosters trust and cooperation from the source, allowing the intelligence officer to gather crucial information more efficiently. To do this, there are several aspects to consider, including privacy and security, comfort of the source, and managing potential distractions.

A. Privacy & Security

Confidentiality and security are essential elements of the face-to-face interview environment. The intelligence officer must ensure that the location chosen for the interview is free of unwanted third parties and listening or monitoring devices. A safe and confidential place is necessary for the source to feel comfortable sharing sensitive information with confidence.

The agent must also clearly explain to the source the measures taken to protect his information and assure him that his cooperation will remain confidential. This guarantee of confidentiality strengthens the source's trust in the agent and encourages an open and honest exchange of information.

B. Source comfort

The comfort of the source is a determining factor for the quality of the interview. The agent must create a welcoming and reassuring environment, where the source feels comfortable speaking freely. Friendly gestures, a respectful attitude and attentive listening help to establish a climate of trust conducive to communication.

The agent may also offer drinks or snacks at the source to create a relaxed atmosphere. Considering the source's individual needs and preferences, such as breaks to rest or refresh, can also contribute to their comfort and overall well-being during the interview.

C. Managing potential distractions

During a face-to-face interview, potential distractions can affect the quality of the information exchange. The intelligence officer must be attentive to the environment and anticipate possible distractions, such as background noise, interruptions or outside interference.

It is important to minimize these distractions by choosing a quiet location and turning off cell phones or other devices that may disrupt the interview. By ensuring a calm and disturbing environment, the agent allows the source to fully concentrate on the interview and thus facilitates the exchange of information.

Interview opening and closing techniques

The opening and closing of the interview in HUMINT are key moments to establish a connection with the source and conclude the exchange in a positive way. These techniques are fundamental to building trust and cooperation, while expressing respect and appreciation for the source. In this chapter, we will examine in detail the different strategies to break the ice and make a connection, express gratitude and respect at the end of the interview, as well as allow the source to ask questions.

A. Breaking the ice and making a connection

Breaking the ice at the beginning of the interview is essential to creating a warm and comfortable environment. The intelligence officer can start with friendly greetings, smiles, and gestures of politeness. A brief discussion of non-intelligence topics, such as the weather or recent events, can also help relax the atmosphere and establish an initial connection.

By establishing a connection with the source, the agent shows that they are open and understanding, which encourages the source to feel comfortable sharing information. Active listening techniques, such as nodding or making positive comments, can reinforce this connection and show the source that their words are valued.

B. Express gratitude and respect at the end of the interview

At the close of the interview, it is crucial for the intelligence officer to express gratitude and respect to the source for its cooperation. Sincere expressions of thanks demonstrate to the source that his contribution is appreciated and valued. The agent may express appreciation for the time granted by the source and emphasize the importance of his information for the success of the operation or investigation.

By expressing respect and gratitude, the officer also reinforces the relationship of trust established throughout the interview. The source will feel valued as a partner in the intelligence process, which can pave the way for future collaboration.

C. Give the source the opportunity to ask questions

Finally, it is essential to give the source the opportunity to ask questions at the end of the interview. This practice demonstrates that the intelligence officer is open to two-way communication and values the concerns of the source. The questions asked by the source can also provide additional clarification on some of the information shared, which can be useful for later analysis.

By allowing the source to ask questions, the agent also facilitates the resolution of any misunderstandings or confusions, further strengthening the relationship of trust and respect between the two parties.

Manage sensitive situations during the interview

During an interview, sensitive situations may arise, testing the intelligence officer's ability to maintain effective and respectful communication. In this chapter, we will explore three types of delicate situations and strategies for managing them diligently and professionally.

A. Responding to the reluctance of the source to disclose information

The source is often reluctant to share certain sensitive or confidential information. The intelligence officer must use patience and persuasion to encourage the source to feel confident. An empathetic approach is essential, showing the source that it is listened to and understood.

The officer can explain the importance of the information sought and highlight how it could be beneficial to the source or to the public interest. By showing that the cooperation of the source is valuable and necessary, the agent can overcome reluctance and encourage a more open and sincere exchange of information.

B. Dealing with differences of opinion or disagreements

During the interview, differences of opinion or disagreements may arise between the intelligence officer and the source. In such situations, it is crucial to remain calm and respectful.

The agent can take into account the opinions of the source and consider them carefully. Explaining why these discrepancies may exist and showing interest in the source's perspectives can open up constructive discussions. The goal is not to convince the source to change his mind, but to understand the reasoning and motivations behind his statements.

C. Avoid behaviors that compromise the relationship of trust

It is essential that the agent avoid any behaviour that could compromise the relationship of trust established with the source. This includes not being condescending, critical, or impatient with the source. The agent must respect the limits of the source and not push it to share information it does not wish to disclose.

In addition, the officer must be transparent about the objectives of the interview and not mislead the source or lie to obtain information. Integrity and sincerity are essential to preserve the relationship of trust and guarantee the reliability of the information collected.

Ethics in direct questioning

Ethics plays a fundamental role in direct questioning. To ensure the integrity of the interview process and maintain the confidence of sources, the intelligence officer must adhere to strict ethical principles. In this chapter, we will examine three crucial aspects of ethics in direct interrogation: respect for privacy and confidentiality, protection of the rights and dignity of sources, and integrity and honesty in the collection of information.

A. Privacy and confidentiality

Privacy and confidentiality are fundamental principles in direct questioning. The intelligence officer must ensure that the personal information of the source is treated with the utmost discretion. This includes limiting access to the information collected and ensuring that only authorized persons have access to that data.

The agent must also obtain informed consent from the source before collecting sensitive personal information. If the source expresses concerns about privacy, the agent should take them seriously and implement measures to protect their information.

B. Protection of the rights and dignity of sources

In direct questioning, the intelligence officer must attach paramount importance to the protection of the rights and dignity of sources. This means treating every source with respect, without discrimination or prejudice. The agent must not exploit or manipulate the vulnerability of the source to obtain information.

In addition, the agent must be aware of the legitimate rights of the source, such as the right to remain silent or refuse to answer certain questions. It is essential to respect these rights and not to exert undue pressure on the source for answers.

D. Integrity and honesty in gathering information

Integrity and honesty are essential values in gathering information in HUMINT. The intelligence officer must undertake to report the information faithfully and accurately, without distortion or exaggeration. The deliberate manipulation of information or the presentation of false information are unacceptable practices that undermine the credibility of the entire intelligence process.

In addition, the officer must be transparent about the purpose of the interview and not conceal his or her real intentions. The source must be informed of the purpose of the collection of the information and the context in which it will be used.

Analyze and verify the information obtained

Once information has been gathered during interrogation, the next step is to analyze and verify it to assess its credibility and reliability. This phase is critical to ensure that the information collected is relevant, accurate and useful for intelligence operations. In this chapter, we will examine three essential aspects of the analysis and verification of the information obtained: assessing the credibility of sources, cross-referencing data with other sources of information, and preventing misinterpretation.

A. Assessment of the credibility of sources

The assessment of the credibility of the sources is a crucial step in the process of analyzing the information obtained in HUMINT. The intelligence officer must carefully consider the reliability of each source based on several factors. These factors include the background check of the source, its potential access to the information sought, its motivations for providing information, and the consistency of its statements with other sources of information.

The agent should also consider any possible bias or conflict of interest on the part of the source, as this could affect the credibility of the information provided. The combination of these elements allows the agent to determine whether the information obtained is trustworthy and can be used to make informed decisions.

B. Cross-referencing of data with other sources of information

To enhance the reliability of the information gathered, the intelligence officer must cross-reference the data obtained with other available sources of information. This includes information from other human, technical or open intelligence (OSINT) sources. The cross-referencing of data makes it possible to check the consistency and concordance of the information, as well as to identify any inconsistencies or contradictions.

The agent must be careful not to rely solely on one source to make important decisions. Cross-referencing information from multiple sources provides a more complete and reliable overview of the situation.

C . Prevention of misinterpretation

The interpretation of the information collected may be subject to potential errors. To avoid misinterpretation, the intelligence officer must be objective and cautious in his analysis. He must avoid jumping to hasty conclusions or drawing inferences not supported by solid evidence.

Clear and accurate communication of information is also essential to prevent misunderstandings or distortions of meaning. The agent should be attentive to the nuances of the language used by the source and be sure to ask additional questions to clarify any ambiguity.

Develop interrogation skills

To become a HUMINT interrogation expert, it is essential for the intelligence officer to continually develop his skills and improve his techniques. In this chapter, we will examine three key strategies for strengthening interrogation skills: regular practice based on training scenarios, soliciting feedback from other professionals, and maintaining a watch on new techniques and practices.

A. Practice regularly and rely on training scenarios

Regular practice is fundamental to refining interrogation skills. The intelligence officer must practice frequently in realistic scenarios to develop his ability to conduct effective interviews. This can be done within training teams or training scenarios specifically designed to simulate real-life situations.

Training scenarios allow the agent to confront various situations and become familiar with complex contexts. This includes managing recalcitrant sources, negotiating with hostile individuals, or gathering information in stressful environments. These exercises strengthen communication, problem-solving and emotional management skills, which are essential for success in HUMINT.

B. Solicit feedback from other professionals

Seeking feedback and advice from other professionals is a valuable way to improve your interrogation skills. Debriefing sessions with experienced colleagues or trainers allow the agent to benefit from constructive feedback and identify areas for improvement.

Feedback from other professionals can also provide different perspectives and innovative approaches to conducting successful interviews. The exchange of experiences and good practices contributes to enriching the skills of the agent by providing him with new ideas and techniques.

C. Keep abreast of new techniques and practices

Interrogation is an ever-evolving field, with new techniques and practices emerging regularly. The intelligence officer must keep abreast of the latest developments and best practices in HUMINT. This can be accomplished by participating in continuing education, reading specialized books, and attending conferences or webinars on the topic.

The search for new knowledge and skills ensures that the officer remains at the forefront of interrogation advances. This allows it to adapt its methods to changing contexts and to be better prepared to meet future intelligence challenges.

Conclusion on the art of direct interrogation in HUMINT

The art of direct interrogation in HUMINT is a complex and essential discipline in the field of intelligence. Throughout this book, we have explored the multiple aspects that make this skill a major asset for intelligence professionals, whether they are private investigators, police officers, business intelligence consultants or ordinary citizens. From the careful preparation of the interview, to the analysis and verification of the information obtained, to the development of interpersonal skills and ethics in conducting interviews, each step of the process was thoroughly addressed.

Direct questioning in HUMINT is above all an art of communication. It is the ability to build trust with a human source and gather crucial information through direct face-to-face interaction. To achieve this goal, the intelligence officer must cultivate strong interpersonal skills, such as active listening, reformulation, and emotional management. These skills help to connect with the source and create an environment conducive to cooperation.

Preparing for the interview is a fundamental step in maximizing the chances of success. The officer must conduct thorough research on the source and the context in which it operates. Understanding the motivations, interests and concerns of the source is essential to adapt the approach and ask the right questions. Careful preparation also helps develop a clear and structured interview plan, ensuring that all relevant information is gathered in an organized manner.

Ethics occupies a central place in the direct interrogation in HUMINT. Respect for privacy, protection of the rights and dignity of sources, and integrity in the collection of information are essential principles to preserve the trust of the source and the credibility of the information gathered. The intelligence officer must act with honesty, transparency and professionalism at all times, avoiding any behavior that could compromise the relationship of trust established.

Managing sensitive situations is also an essential aspect of direct interrogation in HUMINT. The officer must be prepared to deal with intense emotions, address sensitive topics, and handle differences of opinion or disagreement. Empathy, calmness and respect are essential to maintaining the climate of trust necessary for effective communication.

Once information is obtained, analysis and verification play a crucial role in assessing its credibility and reliability. The agent must cross-reference the data with other sources of information to verify its consistency and accuracy. Preventing misinterpretation is also essential to ensure that information is interpreted objectively and accurately.

Developing interrogation skills is an ongoing process that requires constant commitment. Regular practice based on training scenarios allows the agent to build capacity and become familiar with different contexts. Seeking feedback from other professionals and seeking advice allows you to gain fresh perspectives and improve your approaches.

Finally, keeping abreast of new techniques and practices is essential to stay at the forefront of the evolution of the field of interrogation in HUMINT. The constant search for new knowledge and skills ensures that the officer is better prepared to meet future challenges and contribute effectively to intelligence operations.

In conclusion, direct questioning in HUMINT is a complex art that relies on communication, trust and ethics. It is an essential skill for obtaining valuable information and making informed intelligence decisions. By developing strong interpersonal skills, rigorously preparing, acting ethically and continuing to develop, the intelligence officer can become an expert in the delicate art of direct questioning in HUMINT. This expertise is an invaluable asset to those seeking to address the complex challenges of the intelligence world, whether as a security professional, business intelligence consultant or private citizen eager to contribute to a safer and more informed world.

2. Collection of testimonies: Obtain written or oral statements from individuals regarding specific events.

The collection of testimonies is a crucial step in the collection of information in HUMINT. Once you have conducted the interviews with witnesses, it is important to take steps to record and transcribe these statements, classify them in an organized manner and protect them to ensure their integrity and accessibility when they are necessary for further investigations or research. Here are some practical steps to complete these tasks:

1. Recording of testimonies:

Handwritten notes: During the interview, take detailed handwritten notes by listening carefully to the witness. Write down important details, dates, places and people mentioned, as well as answers to key questions. Be sure to use a dedicated pen and notebook to avoid confusion.

Audio recording: With the consent of the witness, you can use an audio recorder to capture the full interview. This allows for an accurate recording of statements, but remember to respect confidentiality and inform the witness of the recording beforehand.

2. Transcript of testimony:

After the interview, take the time to transcribe your handwritten notes or audio recording. Transcription ensures that you have a clear and organized version of the witness' statements. You can do this yourself or delegate this task to a qualified assistant.

When transcribing, be sure to remain faithful to the words of the witness and to avoid any interpretation or addition of personal information.

3. Classification and organization:

Create a consistent filing system to organize the testimonials collected. You can use physical folders or digital folders depending on your preferences.

Organize testimonials in chronological order, by theme, or by relevance for easy access and subsequent research.

Label each testimonial with information such as date, witness name, interview topic, and any other relevant data for quick identification.

4. Protection of testimony:

Keep testimonials in a safe and confidential location to prevent leakage or unauthorized use. If you're working as a team, share testimonials only with members who need access for their work. If necessary, be sure to protect the identity of witnesses for security or confidentiality reasons.

5. Use of Testimonials:

When using testimonies for investigations or research, be sure to cite sources correctly and respect the confidentiality of witnesses. Cross-reference testimonials with other sources of information to verify their accuracy and strengthen their credibility.

By following these steps, you will be able to record, transcribe, classify and protect the testimonies collected effectively and ethically. These statements can provide crucial information for intelligence decision-making and contribute to the overall understanding of the specific events being studied.

3. Informant Recruitment: Identifying and convincing individuals to provide confidential information in exchange for certain incentives.

The recruitment of informants is a key step in intelligence, aimed at identifying and persuading individuals to disclose confidential information in exchange for specific incentives. This strategic practice relies on relationships of trust, discretion and reciprocity to obtain valuable and sensitive information. In this quest for information, building strong relationships and providing tailored benefits play a key role in convincing potential informants to cooperate with intelligence officials.

I. Introduction to Informant Recruitment

A. Definition of the informant and his/her role

An informant is a person who, voluntarily or involuntarily, provides confidential information to a person or organisation. In the intelligence context, an informant plays a crucial role in providing valuable and sensitive information on specific topics, organizations or activities. Informants can be internal sources, such as employees or members of an organization, or external sources that have access to strategic information.

The role of the informant is to share relevant and confidential information with intelligence officials. This information can contribute to informed decision-making, threat prevention, resolution of investigations, or understanding of complex situations. The recruitment of informants is a common practice in the field of intelligence and is based on relationships of trust, discretion and reciprocity.

B. Importance of recruiting informants in intelligence

The recruitment of informants is essential to obtain sensitive, confidential and often difficult to obtain information by other means. Informants may have access to internal, secret or strategic information to which intelligence agencies or organizations would not otherwise have access. They may be eyewitnesses to important events, have in-depth knowledge of specific topics, or be able to provide information about the intentions or activities of potentially dangerous individuals or groups.

Recruiting informants can be an effective way to gather information in real time, allowing intelligence officials to respond quickly to emerging threats. Informants can also help identify vulnerabilities, weaknesses or illegal practices within an organization, which may be essential to protect national security, economic interests or public safety.

However, the recruitment of informants also raises ethical and practical questions. Intelligence officials must ensure that the recruitment and use of informants complies with applicable laws and regulations, protects the rights and safety of informants, and prevents misuse or unethical use of the information provided. Successful recruitment is based on relationships of trust, respect and mutual benefit between the informant and intelligence officials, ensuring fruitful and ethical cooperation.

II. Identification of potential candidates

A. Profiles of Informants Sought

For the recruitment of informants, it is essential to define the profiles of the people sought according to the specific information needed. Profiles may vary depending on intelligence objectives, areas of interest or ongoing investigations. Some examples of profiles of wanted informants could include employees of targeted companies, members of suspicious organizations, experts in strategic areas or individuals with access to sensitive information.

B. Sources to identify potential candidates

There are different sources to identify potential candidates as informants. These sources can be used discreetly and strategically to identify individuals who might be interested in providing confidential information in exchange for inducements. Some potential sources include:

Human contact: Personal and professional relationships can be leveraged to identify individuals who might be able to provide useful information.

Social media: Social media platforms can offer insights into users' interests, affiliations, or specific knowledge, which can be helpful in spotting potential candidates.

Internal sources: In some situations, internal members of an organization may be identified as potential candidates to provide confidential information about their employer or internal activities.

Public sources: Public information such as press reports, academic publications or professional presentations may reveal individuals who may be in possession of sought-after information.

Trusted references: Existing informants or trusted sources can provide references or recommendations to identify potential new candidates.

By using these sources prudently and ethically, intelligence officials can target and identify potential candidates for recruitment as informants, helping to enrich their information base and achieve their intelligence goals.

III. Approach and communication with candidates

A. Establish discreet initial contact

When approaching potential candidates for recruitment as informants, it is essential to proceed in a discreet and confidential manner. Avoid disclosing the purpose of recruitment at the outset and identify the most appropriate ways to establish initial contact. This may involve face-to-face meetings, encrypted communications, or trusted intermediaries to preserve confidentiality.

C. Present the benefits of the informant partnership

To convince candidates to cooperate as informants, it is crucial to clearly present the benefits of the partnership. Highlight why their collaboration is valuable and how it can contribute to important goals, such as national security, threat prevention, or the protection of vital interests. Also highlight potential benefits for them, such as protecting their identity, financial incentives, the opportunity to contribute positively to important issues, or the satisfaction of serving a just cause.

C. Maintaining confidentiality and security

Privacy and security are crucial aspects when approaching and communicating with potential candidates. Be sure to provide guarantees to protect their identity and personal information. Avoid sharing sensitive details until you have established a certain level of trust with the candidate. Use secure and encrypted means of communication if necessary to protect the confidentiality of exchanges.

How intelligence officials approach and communicate with potential candidates can have a significant impact on their decision to cooperate as informants. A discreet, clearly reasoned and secure approach can help build strong relationships of trust and ensure the successful collaboration of these key players in the collection of confidential information.

IV. Convincing informants to cooperate

A. Identify candidates' motivations and interests

To convince candidates to cooperate as informants, it is essential to understand their motivations and interests. Each individual may be motivated by different factors, such as loyalty to a cause, desire to make a positive difference, interest in national security, financial need, sense of justice, or a desire to protect their community or loved ones. By identifying these motivations, intelligence officials can tailor their approach and offer to engage and collaborate with potential candidates.

B. Offer appropriate incentives

Incentives play an important role in encouraging informants to cooperate in a sustainable manner. These incentives may vary depending on the needs and expectations of the candidates. Some common incentives may include financial compensation, protection of identity, immunity or reduction of sentence for individuals facing legal problems, recognition and gratitude for their contribution, or the opportunity to actively participate in the resolution of important issues. It is crucial that the incentives offered are tailored to each potential informant and remain ethical and legal.

It is up to the agent to target the recognition to its source. For this, it must carry out a preliminary research work on its objective.

C. Creating a climate of trust and empathy

Trust is the foundation of successful collaboration with informants. Intelligence officials must build trust by being honest, transparent and reliable in their interactions with candidates. They must also show empathy by understanding the concerns, fears and needs of potential informants. By creating an environment where informants feel understood, respected and safe, intelligence officials can foster sincere and lasting cooperation.

The ability to convince informants to cooperate is an essential aspect of successful informant recruitment. By identifying their motivations, offering appropriate incentives, and building trust and empathy, intelligence officials can build strong partnerships with key informants, helping to gather confidential information relevant to intelligence operations.

VI. Informant Relationship Management

A. Maintain open communication channels

Successful informant management relies on maintaining open and effective communication channels. It is essential to establish regular and secure means of communication to keep in touch with informants. This can include face-to-face meetings, secure email exchanges, or the use of encrypted messaging platforms. By maintaining fluid communication, intelligence officials can ensure that they are informed of relevant developments and respond quickly to the needs of informants.

Here are some types of channels that can be used for communication with informants:

1. Face-to-face meetings: Face-to-face meetings allow for direct and confidential communication, fostering greater mutual understanding and exchange of information.

2. Telephone: Telephone conversations can be used to maintain regular contact with informants, while ensuring a certain geographical distance to keep them safe.

3. Secure emails: The use of encrypted and secure emails allows for confidential communication, protecting sensitive information exchanged.

4. Encrypted messaging platforms: Secure messaging applications, using encryption protocols, can be set up to ensure the confidentiality of exchanges.

5. Dead mailboxes: This system allows informants to leave information without having to meet face-to-face, reducing the risk of compromise.

6. Pre-set signals: Pre-established signals and codes can be used to communicate discreetly in situations where safety is paramount.

7. Secure Websites: Secure online spaces may be created to exchange information securely.

8. Intermediate communications: The use of trusted intermediaries can help separate the source of the intelligence agency's information, thereby enhancing the protection of the informant.

9. Encrypted communication apps: Some instant messaging apps offer end-to-end encryption features to ensure the confidentiality of exchanges.

10. Secure Radio Channel: In some cases, a secure radio communication channel may be established for quick and confidential exchanges.

It is essential to choose the communication channels according to the level of confidentiality required and the security of the information exchanged. Intelligence officials must ensure that confidentiality is maintained and the identity of informants is protected, using the channels most appropriate to each situation.

B. Recognize and reward the contributions of informants

Recognizing and rewarding informants' contributions is essential to keep them motivated and engaged. Intelligence officials should express gratitude to informants for the information provided and the impact of their cooperation. The rewards can be diverse, ranging from financial benefits to protecting their safety and anonymity, to sincere words of thanks. Regular recognition of informants' efforts strengthens the relationship of trust and encourages them to continue to collaborate.

C. Overcoming challenges and potential risks

Managing relationships with informants can be complex and involves challenges and potential risks. Intelligence officials must be aware of these challenges and prepare to deal with them. Some common challenges include the risk of informant security being compromised, managing expectations on both sides, the need to maintain the confidentiality of shared information, and protecting sensitive sources. Open and honest communication with informants can help anticipate and overcome these challenges.

By effectively managing relationships with informants, maintaining open channels of communication, recognizing and rewarding their contributions, and overcoming potential challenges, intelligence officials can build strong relationships of trust and partnership with their informants. These successful relationships contribute to the collection of valuable information and the achievement of intelligence objectives in an ethical and effective manner.

VII. Ethics and Respect in Informant Recruitment

A. Respect for the rights and dignity of informants

The recruitment of informants must be carried out with strict respect for the rights and dignity of these individuals. Intelligence officials must recognize that informants are people with their basic rights and autonomy. They must obtain the informed consent of informants and ensure that they fully understand the implications of their cooperation. It is essential never to force, manipulate or exploit informants to obtain information.

B. Avoiding misuse or unethical use of information

Information provided by informants must be used ethically, legally and responsibly. Intelligence officials must ensure that the information collected is not used to harm individuals, violate their privacy, or compromise their security. Sensitive information must be protected and must not be used for unauthorized or unethical purposes. The use of information provided by reporting persons should be limited to legitimate intelligence, national security or threat prevention purposes.

Informants recruiters need to be aware of the impact of their actions on the lives and safety of informants. They must act with integrity, honesty and transparency throughout the recruitment and management process of informants. By respecting the rights and dignity of informants and avoiding any misuse or unethical use of information, intelligence officers can ensure an ethical and responsible approach to the recruitment of informants. This helps to preserve mutual trust and strengthen fruitful relationships with these key players in the collection of confidential information.

VIII. Conclusion on the importance of informant recruitment and its role in intelligence.

The recruitment of informants is central to the intelligence field, playing a critical role in the collection of confidential information and informed decision-making. This strategic practice relies on building trusting relationships with individuals willing to share sensitive information in exchange for appropriate incentives. In this conclusion, we will highlight the importance of informant recruitment, its key role in intelligence, and the ethical and operational challenges that accompany it.

The recruitment of informants is crucial to access information that is inaccessible by other means. These informants can be internal sources, such as employees of target organizations, or external sources with privileged access to strategic information. They provide valuable and up-to-date information, contributing to the early detection of threats, understanding complex situations, resolving investigations, and making informed decisions. Confidential information obtained through these informants can play a critical role in protecting national security, economic interests, and preventing crime or malicious behavior.

The role of informants in intelligence is not limited to data collection. They can also offer a human perspective on the events and actions of targeted individuals or groups. Their in-depth understanding of the environment in which they operate and their interactions with other actors can provide valuable insights to assess the intentions and motivations of the intended targets. With their contribution, intelligence officials can better anticipate emerging threats, develop more effective strategies, and take preventive measures to protect national interests.

However, recruiting informants is not without its challenges. The recruitment process requires the establishment of secure and discreet communication channels, as well as approaches adapted to each individual. It also requires a thorough understanding of candidates' motivations and interests to encourage them to cooperate voluntarily and sustainably. Managing relationships with informants requires ongoing communication, appropriate rewards for collaboration, and managing potential risks related to their security and privacy.

In addition, the recruitment of informants raises important ethical questions. Intelligence officials must act with integrity, respecting the rights and dignity of informants, and avoiding any misuse or unethical use of the information provided. The informed consent of informants should be obtained, and the benefits and risks of their cooperation should be clearly explained. Protecting their identity and security is crucial to keeping them safe and encouraging their continued engagement.

In the complex intelligence environment, the recruitment of informants remains a valuable tool for obtaining sensitive and relevant information. However, it must be approached responsibly and ethically. Intelligence officials must constantly assess the benefits and risks associated with recruiting informants and ensure that their actions comply with applicable laws and ethical standards.

In conclusion, the recruitment of informants is a fundamental aspect of intelligence, contributing significantly to the collection of confidential information and the protection of national interests. Informants play a key role in providing critical information, human perspectives and helping to make informed decisions. However, this complex process requires an ethical approach, respectful of the rights of informants, and the implementation of security measures to ensure their protection. By navigating with integrity and prudence in recruiting informants, intelligence officials can strengthen their ability to address security challenges and emerging threats in an ever-changing world.

4. Networking: Establish and maintain relationships with trusted contacts to obtain information regularly.

Networking, or networking, is an essential practice in the field of intelligence, aimed at establishing and maintaining relationships with reliable contacts to obtain information regularly. This strategic approach is based on building networks of trust, gathering relevant information and creating strategic alliances. In this section, we will explore the importance of networking in the context of intelligence, methods for establishing and maintaining effective relationships, and the benefits and challenges of this practice.

I. The Importance of Intelligence Networking

Networking plays a crucial role in intelligence by providing access to diverse and specialized sources of information. Contacts within reliable networks can provide information from different perspectives, industries or geographical areas, helping to broaden the scope of the information collected. Through networking, intelligence officials can gain real-time insights, anticipate emerging threats, understand geopolitical and economic dynamics, and better assess the intentions of key players.

In addition, networking allows access to confidential information that would not be available by other means. Established contacts may have access to inside information, specialized analysis or internal reports, which can be crucial for informed decision-making. The information obtained through networking can complement that collected by other intelligence methods, thus enhancing the quality and relevance of the analyses.

Networking also fosters understanding of cultures, social norms and local specificities. Contacts made in different geographic or cultural contexts can provide key contextual information, which is essential for correctly interpreting the information collected. These people-to-people relationships also facilitate communication and cooperation with international partners, thereby strengthening multilateral intelligence collaboration.

II. Methods for establishing networking relationships

A. Identify networking targets:

The first step to building effective networking relationships is to identify potential targets. This may include experts in strategic areas, key sources within targeted organizations, reputable analysts, diplomats, academics or industry professionals. The diversity of targets provides access to varied and complementary information.

B. Participate in professional and social events:

Business events, conferences, trade shows, seminars and social gatherings are valuable opportunities to meet new people and make contacts. These opportunities allow for informal interactions and foster trusting relationships.

C. Use social networks and professional platforms:

Professional social networks such as LinkedIn can be powerful tools for networking and interacting with professionals from various industries. Participating in relevant online discussion groups can also facilitate the exchange of information and knowledge.

D. Collaborate with trusted partners:

Working with trusted partners, such as foreign intelligence agencies or international organizations, helps strengthen intelligence networks and exchange information securely.

III. Maintain effective networking relationships

Maintaining regular communication with established contacts is essential to preserve the relationship and obtain up-to-date information. Intelligence officials must ensure that they stay in touch, exchange relevant information, and meet the needs of their contacts.

A. Stay informed of each contact's topics of interest:

To maintain fruitful networking relationships, it is important to learn about the topics of interest of each contact. This knowledge allows for meaningful discussions and demonstrates genuine interest in each other's concerns.

B. Respect the confidentiality and limits of each contact:

Intelligence networking often involves sharing sensitive information. It is essential to respect the confidentiality of each contact and not to exceed the limits set by them. Mutual trust is crucial to maintaining an effective networking relationship.

IV. The Benefits of Intelligence Networking

1. Access to diversified information: Networking provides access to information from diverse and specialized sources, thus improving the quality and relevance of the information collected.

2. Anticipating emerging threats: Established contacts can provide real-time information, allowing intelligence officials to anticipate emerging threats and take preventive action.

3. Understanding geopolitical and economic dynamics: Networking fosters an understanding of cultures, social norms and local specificities, which are essential for correctly interpreting the information collected.

4. Strengthening international collaboration: Networking facilitates communication and cooperation with international partners, thereby strengthening multilateral intelligence collaboration.

5. Discreet observation: Discreetly monitoring individuals or locations for undetected information.

Discreet observation is a fundamental technique in the field of intelligence, allowing to discreetly monitor individuals, places or activities to obtain information without being detected. This strategic approach is based on discretion, vigilance and mastery of observation techniques. In this section, we will explore the importance of discreet observation in the intelligence context, the methods and equipment used to carry out this technique, and the challenges and ethical considerations that accompany it.

I. The Importance of Covert Surveillance in Intelligence

Discreet observation plays a crucial role in gathering intelligence in a non-intrusive manner. This technique allows intelligence officials to gather valuable information without alerting targeted subjects. It is particularly useful in counterintelligence operations, criminal investigations, surveillance of suspicious groups, as well as in identifying potentially threatening behavior or activity.

Discreet observation provides first-hand, real-time information and provides accurate details about the activities and interactions of the individuals being monitored. This approach provides unique insight into social dynamics, lifestyle habits, connections between individuals, and behaviours that may be beyond other methods of information gathering.

In addition, discreet observation may contribute to the confirmation or refutation of information gathered by other means of intelligence, such as interception of communications, analysis of data or collection of testimony. It also detects behaviours or changes in interest that could be significant in the context of an investigation or intelligence mission.

II. Discrete observation methods

A. Foot surveillance:

Foot-based surveillance involves the physical presence of a discreet observer on the ground. The observer discreetly follows the targeted subjects, avoiding being noticed and adapting to their pace and behavior. This method allows for a more detailed observation of the social interactions, movements and activities of the individuals being monitored.

B. Static Monitoring:

Static surveillance involves discreetly observing a fixed location, such as a residence, office, or site of interest. The observer can use optical observation devices, such as binoculars or observation cameras, to gather information remotely without being detected.

C. Mobile Surveillance:

Mobile surveillance involves the use of discrete vehicles to discreetly track individuals or moving vehicles. This method makes it possible to track the movements of targeted subjects over greater distances and to adapt to rapid changes in their route.

D. Electronic Monitoring:

Electronic surveillance uses electronic devices such as CCTV cameras, voice recorders or geolocation devices to collect information remotely. This method can be used in addition to other discrete observation methods.

III. Equipment and techniques used for discreet observation

A. Observation cameras:

Observation cameras are essential equipment for remote surveillance. They can be concealed in ordinary objects such as watches, buttons, pens or glasses, to allow discreet observation without arousing suspicion.

B. Night observation binoculars:

Night observation binoculars allow effective observation in low light conditions or in total darkness. They are particularly useful for night surveillance.

C. Discreet listening devices:

Discreet listening devices, such as voice recorders or concealed microphones, can be used to collect conversations and verbal information without being detected.

D. Concealment techniques:

Observers must master concealment techniques to avoid detection by the subjects being monitored. This may include using discreet clothing, regularly changing appearance, using blankets or disguises, and adapting to the environment to go unnoticed.

E. Counter-surveillance techniques:

Observers should also be aware of the counter-surveillance techniques used by targeted subjects to detect surveillance. They must take steps to avoid detection and to protect their coverage.

IV. Challenges and Ethical Considerations of Discreet Compliance

Discreet observation presents significant challenges and ethical considerations. Observers must be careful not to violate the privacy of the individuals under surveillance, avoiding gathering information that is not relevant to the intelligence mission. They must also comply with applicable laws and regulations regarding the collection of sensitive information.

Observation can require hours of patience and determination, as well as an ability to stay focused in demanding and sometimes dangerous situations. Observers must exercise a high degree of discretion to avoid compromising their coverage and endangering their safety.

It is also essential to continuously assess the benefits and risks of discreet observation, ensuring that the information gathered justifies the use of this technique. A balanced and responsible approach is needed to avoid any abusive or unethical use of this method of intelligence.

6. Background research: Review individuals' records and histories for relevant information.

Background research plays a crucial role in gathering information about targeted individuals. It allows intelligence officers to trace the professional, educational and personal backgrounds of those targeted, as well as their past and present affiliations. This technique provides key information about criminal history, potentially dangerous associations, past activities, and family ties.

Background research is used in a variety of intelligence contexts. In criminal investigations, it helps identify potential suspects, trace their movements and interactions, and understand the motivations behind their actions. In the field of military intelligence, it can detect individuals with links to extremist groups or terrorist organizations. In national security investigations, it can be used to identify individuals potentially vulnerable to blackmail or manipulation.

Before engaging with a potential source, it is essential to conduct a thorough investigation of their background and affiliations to ensure their reliability and credibility.

7. Neighborhood survey: Interviewing neighbors and people close to a target to gather information about their behavior and activities.

Neighborhood investigation is an essential technique in the field of intelligence, collecting relevant information about a target's behavior and activities by interviewing its neighbors and people close to its immediate environment. This strategic approach relies on the use of local human sources to obtain accurate and reliable details about a targeted person's lifestyle, social interactions and movements.

The information obtained through the neighbourhood survey can provide important insights in a variety of intelligence contexts. In criminal investigations, this technique can be used to trace the movements and activities of a suspect, as well as to collect testimonies about suspicious behavior or relevant events. In counterintelligence operations, neighborhood investigation can help identify individuals potentially involved in espionage activities or contacts with foreign agents. In the field of national security, this technique can be used to assess potential threats and suspicious activities in a given environment.

The method of the neighbourhood survey may vary depending on the situation and specific constraints. Intelligence officials may opt for in-person interviews, telephone interviews, or even anonymous surveys to protect the identity of informants. Discreet observation of the target's activities and interactions with neighbors can also be used to supplement the information obtained through interviews.

However, the neighborhood survey raises important ethical considerations. Intelligence officials must ensure that this investigation is conducted in a discreet, confidential and respectful manner for the privacy of witnesses. The informed consent of witnesses must be obtained before gathering information, and witnesses must be given the opportunity to refuse to testify if they so wish. It is also crucial to avoid manipulation or influence on witness responses, in order to ensure the integrity and reliability of the information collected.

In conclusion, neighborhood investigation is a powerful tool in the field of intelligence, allowing to obtain crucial information about the behavior and activities of a target by interviewing its neighbors and people close to its immediate environment. This technique relies on the exploitation of local human sources and can be used in a variety of intelligence contexts, including criminal investigations, counterintelligence operations, and national security. However, its use requires an ethical and responsible approach to preserve the rights and dignity of witnesses, as well as to comply with applicable laws and regulations. By navigating the neighborhood investigation with integrity and professionalism, intelligence officials can enhance their ability to gather relevant information while safeguarding national interests in an ethical and responsible manner.

It is important to emphasize that neighbourhood investigation is a technique reserved for professionals approved by the State, such as judicial police officers or duly authorized intelligence agents. This practice must be carried out by trained and empowered individuals, as it involves the collection of sensitive information about individuals and their activities. As such, the neighbourhood survey is subject to strict rules and ethical considerations to ensure respect for individuals' fundamental rights and the protection of their privacy.

Neighborhood investigation is a sensitive activity that requires a thorough understanding of intelligence, personal data protection and privacy laws and regulations. Licensed professionals are trained to conduct this investigation responsibly, avoiding misuse of the information gathered and maintaining the confidentiality of witnesses.

In addition, neighbourhood surveys must be carried out within the framework of an appropriate legal procedure, respecting the authorizations and warrants required by law. This approach ensures that the information collected is admissible in court, where appropriate, and helps prevent any violation of the rights of the individuals concerned.

It is important to stress that any unauthorized attempt to conduct a neighbourhood survey can be illegal and result in severe legal consequences. Only licensed and authorized professionals are allowed to use this technique as part of their legitimate work and in compliance with the legal framework.

8. Reporting: Write detailed reports on information gathered from sources.

Reporting is an essential intelligence skill, allowing for accurate and detailed recording of information gathered from sources. To do this, intelligence professionals must adopt the following techniques:

1. Accuracy: Reports should be clear, concise and accurate. They must faithfully transcribe the information collected without subjective interpretation.

2. Objectivity: Editors should avoid value judgments or personal opinions to ensure the objectivity of the accounts.

3. Structure: Reports should follow a logical and coherent structure, with an introduction, thematic sections and a conclusion.

4. Clarity: Information should be presented in a comprehensible manner, using plain language and avoiding complex technical terms.

5. Relevance: Only relevant information should be included in the report, focusing on items of value to the intelligence objective.

6. Verification: Before finalizing the report, editors should verify the accuracy of the information and ensure consistency with other sources.

7. Security: Reports must be treated confidentially and protected from unauthorized access.

8. Language and style: The choice of language and style should be appropriate to the report's target audience, whether intelligence officials, policy makers or other stakeholders.

By adopting these writing techniques, intelligence professionals can produce high-quality reports, providing reliable and relevant information for informed decision-making.

9. Search for information in trade publications: Obtain relevant information in journals, newspapers or specialized documents

The search for information in specialized publications is a fundamental intelligence technique, making it possible to obtain relevant and up-to-date information from journals, newspapers and specialized documents. This strategic approach offers privileged access to a wealth of valuable information, often publicly available, but overlooked by many analysts. Indeed, it is estimated that nearly 90% of the information sought can be found in these sources accessible to the general public.

I. The Importance of Intelligence Publications

Specialized publications, whether academic, scientific, industrial, or in the field of security, represent a rich and diversified source of information. They cover a multitude of topics, ranging from technological advances to geopolitical analyses to economic and industrial developments. These sources offer an informed and expert perspective on specific topics, making them an invaluable resource for intelligence professionals.

II. Methods for searching for information in specialized publications

A. Online searches: Online databases, journal archives and specialized websites are essential tools for conducting effective searches of trade publications. Academic search engines and digital libraries also offer easy access to a wide variety of sources.

B. Analysis of scientific journals: Scientific journals are an invaluable source of information on technological advances, medical innovations, research studies and trends in various scientific fields.

C. Media monitoring: Regular access to newspapers and news publications keeps abreast of geopolitical developments, international incidents, changes in government policy and global crises.

D. Analysis of industry publications: Industrial journals provide crucial information on economic trends, investments, mergers and acquisitions and technological innovations in specific industries.

III. The use of information from specialized intelligence publications

A. Trend analysis: Information from specialized publications can identify emerging trends in various fields, which is essential for anticipating economic, technological or political changes.

B. Identification of key actors: Trade publications often reveal key players in different sectors, such as opinion leaders, experts, policy makers and major economic actors.

C. Validation of information: Information obtained from trade publications can serve as a source of validation and corroboration of data collected by other intelligence methods, thereby enhancing the credibility of analyses.

IV. Ethical and Legal Considerations

The use of specialized publications for intelligence purposes must be conducted in accordance with applicable laws and regulations. Although these sources are generally publicly accessible, it is crucial to respect copyright and appropriate citation rules when using information extracted from these publications. In addition, the use of specialized publications to collect sensitive or confidential information requires a careful assessment of risks and ethical implications.

In conclusion, searching for information in specialized publications is a powerful and underutilized intelligence technique. These sources offer a wealth of relevant and up-to-date information on a multitude of topics, facilitating the collection of crucial information for analysis and informed decision-making. Intelligence professionals need to take ownership of this technique by using online research methods, analysis of scientific journals, media monitoring, and the exploitation of industry publications to strengthen their ability to collect reliable and relevant information. While taking advantage of these rich sources of information, it is essential to respect ethical and legal considerations to ensure responsible and compliant use of information obtained in trade publications.

10. Use of indirect sources: Obtaining information from third parties who have knowledge about the target.

The use of indirect sources is a crucial technique in the field of intelligence, making it possible to obtain valuable information from third parties with knowledge about the target. These sources, often referred to as secondary informants, can provide unique insights into the target's behaviour, activities, and relationships. This strategic approach is based on collaboration with individuals or organizations that, although not directly involved in the situation under study, have relevant and reliable information.

I. The Importance of Using Indirect Sources in Intelligence

The use of indirect sources offers several major benefits for intelligence professionals. First, it provides access to information that would otherwise be difficult to obtain, especially when the target is very cautious or difficult to approach directly. In addition, indirect sources can provide objective and unbiased insights, due to their emotional distance from the target. Finally, this approach makes it possible to diversify the sources of information, thus enhancing the reliability and credibility of the data collected.

II. Methods for Using Indirect Sources in Intelligence

Interviews with third parties: Intelligence officials may conduct interviews with individuals or organizations that have indirect knowledge about the target. These interviews can be conducted in person, by telephone or through secure online communications.

Collaboration with partners: Alliances with intelligence partners, such as other government agencies or international organizations, can facilitate access to indirect sources.

Analysis of public data : The analysis of public data, such as news articles, official reports, or online publications, can provide useful information from indirect sources.

Use of cross-referenced information: Information obtained from indirect sources can be used to confirm or cross-reference data collected by other intelligence methods, thereby enhancing the credibility of the analyses.

III. The use of information from indirect sources in intelligence

A. Validation of information: Information provided by indirect sources must be rigorously verified and validated to ensure its accuracy and reliability.

B. Data contextualization: Information gathered from indirect sources should be contextualized and linked to other data to provide comprehensive and informed analysis.

IV. Examples of the Use of Indirect Sources in Intelligence

A. Geopolitical analysis: Diplomats, international relations experts, and academics can provide indirect information about the intentions and actions of foreign actors.

B. Risk assessment: National security officials can rely on private sector analysts to assess potential threats to business and infrastructure security.

C. Economic surveillance: Economic analysts and financial market specialists can provide information on economic trends, mergers and acquisitions and capital flows.

Ethical and legal considerations

The use of indirect sources raises important ethical and legal questions. Intelligence officers must ensure that the use of these sources complies with applicable laws and regulations, including data protection and confidentiality. In addition, indirect informants must be informed of the purpose of the collection of information and give their informed consent to participate in this process.

This strategic approach offers major advantages in terms of access to information, objective perspectives and diversification of sources. However, its use requires rigorous validation of information, appropriate contextualization, and adherence to ethical and legal considerations to ensure responsible information collection in accordance with ethical and legal standards. By effectively exploiting indirect sources, intelligence professionals can enhance their ability to obtain information crucial for analysis and informed decision-making.

11. "Moles" identification: Identify individuals who have infiltrated an organization to provide confidential information.

Identifying "Moles" or individuals infiltrated into an organization is a delicate and crucial task in the field of intelligence. This technique aims to identify individuals who have been recruited or manipulated to provide confidential information to foreign entities, criminal groups or other malicious organizations. Identifying "Moles" is essential to protect national security, the confidentiality of sensitive information, and prevent potential leaks.

To identify "Moles," intelligence professionals often use behavioral analysis techniques, carefully observing behavioral changes, signs of stress, or signs of suspicious behavior in employees. In parallel, a thorough background check of employees is carried out to detect potential links or connections with malicious entities. Discreet and lawful surveillance of employee activities and communications can also provide clues to suspicious behavior, contributing to the identification effort.

Increased employee awareness of the risks of espionage and betrayal is essential to enhance security within the organization. Training programs on "Moles" detection, sensitive information protection, and reporting protocols help raise staff awareness and create a culture of security. By collaborating with security and counterintelligence services, intelligence professionals can share information, get advice, and benefit from additional expertise to identify "Moles."

To enhance security, it is also important to use counterintelligence techniques that can deceive or discourage potential "Moles", making it difficult or risky for them to provide confidential information. Rigorous access and authorization management of sensitive information is also essential to limit the risk of internal espionage and information leaks.

12. Use of hidden recording devices: Capture conversations discreetly to gather information.

The use of hidden recording devices is an intelligence technique that allows conversations to be captured discreetly, without the people involved being aware of it. This strategic approach is often used to gather crucial information in situations where a direct approach would be ineffective or risky. However, the use of such devices raises ethical and legal issues and requires responsible use in accordance with applicable laws.

I. The Importance of Using Intelligence Hidden Recording Devices

Hidden recording devices can be valuable intelligence tools, allowing first-hand information to be obtained without arousing the suspicions of those being monitored. They can be used in various scenarios, such as counterintelligence operations, criminal investigations, sensitive negotiations, or to monitor suspicious individuals in national security cases.

II. Methods of using hidden recording devices

Concealed cameras and microphones: Hidden cameras and microphones can be placed in everyday objects, such as pens, shirt buttons, watches or even furniture, to discreetly capture conversations.

Portable audio and video recorders: Portable audio and video recording devices, such as handheld recorders, can be used to capture conversations while traveling or meeting.

Concealment techniques: Intelligence professionals can use advanced concealment techniques to hide recording devices to ensure their discretion and effectiveness.

III. Ethical and legal considerations

The use of hidden recording devices raises important ethical questions regarding the privacy and confidentiality of registrants. In many countries, recording conversations without prior consent is illegal, except in certain specific circumstances, such as national security operations or criminal investigations authorized by law.

It is essential that intelligence professionals strictly comply with applicable laws and regulations regarding the use of hidden recording devices. They must obtain the necessary authorizations before carrying out such operations and ensure that their use is strictly limited to cases where justified by national security or public interest reasons.

Individuals who use such devices without consent may violate privacy laws and face severe legal consequences. Unauthorized use of hidden recording devices can also lead to a loss of trust in personal and professional relationships, as it compromises the confidentiality of conversations and interactions.

IV. Responsible management and protection of information

Recordings obtained using hidden devices must be treated with the utmost care to prevent leakage or misuse of captured information. Intelligence professionals must ensure that recordings are stored securely and accessible only to authorized individuals.

The responsible management of the information thus obtained is essential to ensure its appropriate use and to protect the privacy of the persons concerned.

In conclusion, the use of hidden recording devices is a powerful but delicate intelligence technique. It can provide valuable information in situations where a direct approach would be ineffective or risky. However, their use raises important ethical and legal issues and requires responsible management in accordance with applicable laws. By adhering to ethical and legal standards, intelligence professionals can use this technique responsibly and effectively contribute to the collection of information crucial to national security and public interests.

13. "Looping back": Return to previous sources for updates or additional information.

Looping back, also known as "backtracking," is an essential technique in intelligence. It involves going back to previous sources for updates or additional information. This strategic approach helps maintain strong relationships with sources, build mutual trust and provide deeper information.

The importance of looping back lies in its ability to update information collected in the past, ensuring its relevance and accuracy. By going back to the sources, we can obtain additional information that enriches the existing data. In addition, looping back strengthens ties with sources, encouraging their continued cooperation and willingness to share relevant information in the future.

To implement looping back, it is essential to regularly plan these returns to the sources according to the sensitivity of the information and the dynamics of the situations monitored. Open and respectful communication with sources is also essential to maintain a relationship of trust. Reiterating the importance of confidentiality of the information exchanged ensures that sources feel confident in sharing sensitive information.

14. Use of "Baiting": Attracting sources by using false information or inducements to trick them into divulging information.

The use of "Baiting" is a controversial intelligence technique that aims to lure sources by using false information or inducements to trick them into divulging information. This strategic approach can be seen as a sharp double sword, as it can yield crucial information, but it also raises important ethical and moral questions.

The importance of "Baiting" lies in its ability to entice sources to reveal information they might otherwise keep secret. By using attractive decoys, such as fake news or enticing offers, intelligence professionals hope to encourage sources to reveal themselves and provide valuable details on sensitive topics.

However, the use of "Baiting" raises significant ethical concerns. Deliberately misleading sources using false information or incitement can be considered manipulative and contrary to fundamental principles of intelligence ethics. It can also undermine the trust of sources and jeopardize long-term relationships between intelligence professionals and their sources.

Moreover, the use of "Baiting" can have negative consequences on the credibility and reputation of intelligence professionals. If these practices are discovered, they can bring the profession into disrepute and undermine public confidence in intelligence agencies.

It is therefore essential that intelligence professionals carry out their work with integrity and responsibility. If the use of "Baiting" is justified in specific situations, it must be conducted with caution and in accordance with the laws and ethical standards in force. Clear and transparent guidelines must be established to guide intelligence practices, and professionals must always consider ethical considerations when using "Baiting" techniques.

15. Search for personal details: Collect personal information about sources to establish links and convince them to cooperate.

Personal details research is an intelligence technique aimed at gathering information about sources to establish links and convince them to cooperate. This strategic approach is based on in-depth knowledge of the targeted individuals, their background, interests, and personal relationships. Using this information, intelligence professionals can develop tailored approaches to build trust with sources and encourage them to share sensitive information.

The importance of researching personal details lies in its ability to personalize interactions with sources. By understanding their concerns, needs and motivations, intelligence professionals can tailor their approach to engage and cooperate effectively from sources. This creates an environment conducive to the exchange of confidential information.

However, the search for personal details also raises ethical and legal questions regarding the privacy of individuals. Intelligence professionals should act with caution and comply with applicable laws and regulations when collecting and using this information.

It is essential to ensure that the search for personal details is carried out in a lawful and ethical manner, and that the rights and dignity of individuals are preserved at all times.

Searching for personal details requires information-gathering skills, but also human qualities such as empathy and active listening. By establishing authentic links with sources, intelligence professionals can earn their trust and encourage mutual cooperation based on respect and understanding.

In conclusion, searching for personal details is a powerful but delicate intelligence technique. It builds strong links with sources and convinces them to cooperate voluntarily. However, it must be exercised with integrity and responsibility, respecting the rights and dignity of individuals. By taking a balanced and respectful approach, intelligence professionals can use the search for personal details effectively and ethically to help gather information critical to national security and public interests.

16. Use of covers: Presenting oneself under a false identity to obtain information from a source without revealing one's true identity.

The use of covers is an intelligence technique that involves presenting oneself under a false identity to obtain information from a source without revealing its true identity. This strategic approach is often used in situations where disclosure of the real identity of the intelligence professional could compromise the security of the operation or jeopardize the cooperation of the source.

The importance of using blankets lies in its ability to protect the identity of the intelligence professional while establishing a relationship of trust with the source. By presenting themselves under a false identity, the intelligence professional can access sensitive or confidential information without arousing the suspicion of the source or unwanted third parties.

However, the use of covers raises important ethical questions regarding the manipulation of the identity and trust of the source. Intelligence professionals must act with integrity and responsibility when using this technique, ensuring that they do not abuse the trust of the source or infringe upon their rights or dignity.

To implement this technique, intelligence professionals must have a credible and well-constructed cover identity. This involves developing a fictional character with consistent backgrounds, interests, and relationships, in order to appear credible in the eyes of the source. It is essential to prepare carefully before coming into contact with the source, anticipating possible questions and knowing the story and personality of the cover perfectly.

Safety is also an essential aspect of using blankets. Intelligence professionals should be aware of the potential risks associated with the use of this technique and take appropriate measures to protect their true identity and cover.

17. Search for professional relationships: Identify business relationships or colleagues of a target to obtain relevant information.

A search for professional relations is an intelligence technique that aims to identify business relationships or colleagues of a target to obtain relevant information. This strategic approach is based on an understanding of the target's professional and social connections, which allows for valuable information about their activities, ongoing projects, alliances, interests and concerns.

The importance of seeking professional relationships lies in its ability to provide key contextual information about the target. By analyzing the target's business relationships and professional interactions, intelligence professionals can gain valuable insight into their activities and connections with other actors in the professional community. This can help to better understand its network of influence, its potential partnerships, or to identify possible vulnerabilities.

To implement this technique, intelligence professionals must have information gathering and data analysis skills. They can use different sources of information such as professional social networks, company registers, company websites, specialized publications, or press releases. By cross-referencing this information, they can draw a more complete picture of the target's professional relationships.

However, the search for professional relationships must be carried out with caution and in compliance with the laws and ethical principles in force. It is essential to ensure that the privacy and rights of individuals are respected, and not to use this technique to collect information in an abusive or intrusive manner.

18. Use of cookies: Install eavesdropping or monitoring devices in target locations to obtain confidential information.

The use of cookies, also known as eavesdropping or surveillance devices, is an intelligence technique that is the subject of much controversy. This strategic approach involves discreetly installing devices in target locations to obtain confidential information without the knowledge of the persons being monitored. While this technique can provide crucial information for national security and public interests, it raises important ethical and legal questions.

I. The Importance of Snitches in Intelligence

The use of cookies may be considered a necessary measure in certain circumstances to obtain crucial information about potential targets. These devices can provide tangible evidence of illegal behaviour or dangerous conspiracies, thereby contributing to the safety and protection of the public.

II. The Different Forms of Cookies

Cookies can take many forms, including wiretapping devices hidden in objects, concealed surveillance cameras, hacking software to access confidential data, and many other techniques. Each type of cookie has specific benefits and risks, and their use must be carefully evaluated according to the context and the laws in force.

III. Ethical and legal challenges

The use of cookies raises many ethical and legal challenges. First, it is crucial to respect the privacy and confidentiality rights of individuals. Surveillance devices must be used proportionately and in compliance with privacy laws.

Second, it is essential to ensure that information collected through cookies is used only for legitimate intelligence and national security purposes. Intelligence professionals must ensure that the data obtained is treated with the utmost care and in accordance with privacy rules.

It is essential to remember that the use of cookies, also known as eavesdropping or surveillance devices, is strictly prohibited for civilians in most jurisdictions. These devices are subject to strict privacy laws and their use without legal permission may result in criminal penalties. Snitches are reserved for duly authorized intelligence professionals and law enforcement for legitimate and lawful investigations. It is paramount that civilians respect these laws and refrain from any unlawful use of these devices, in order to preserve the confidentiality and privacy of individuals and to ensure the responsible and ethical use of surveillance technologies.

IV. The importance of oversight and accountability

To mitigate the risks associated with the use of cookies, it is imperative to put in place a system of supervision and accountability. Intelligence operations using surveillance devices must be rigorously supervised, and their use must be justified and documented.

V. The balance between security and respect for individual rights

The use of cookies requires a delicate balance between the imperatives of national security and respect for individual rights. Intelligence professionals must exercise judgment and integrity when deciding to use this technique, carefully weighing the associated benefits and risks.

In conclusion, the use of cookies is a controversial technique in the field of intelligence, which can provide crucial intelligence while raising important ethical and legal questions. Intelligence professionals must carry out their work with integrity, respecting the privacy and confidentiality rights of individuals. They must also ensure that the use of cookies is proportionate and complies with applicable laws. By taking a balanced and accountable approach, intelligence professionals can use this technique effectively and ethically to contribute to the collection of information for national security and public interest.

19. Disguise: Blending into a specific environment to collect information without attracting attention.

Blending into a specific environment through disguise requires a methodical and precise approach. Here are some concrete tips to blend into an environment using disguise:

Environmental Scan: Before dressing up, carefully observe the environment you will be in. Take note of typical local dress, hairstyles, accessories, and social behaviors. This observation will allow you to choose the right disguise and adopt an adapted behavior.

Choice of costume: Select clothing that matches those worn by local people. Avoid outfits that might make you stand out or attract attention. Opt for neutral, simple and discreet clothing, which will allow you to blend in with the crowd.

Use makeup and accessories: If necessary, use makeup to subtly alter your appearance. This may include changing hair color, contact lenses to change eye color, or using prosthetics to change facial shape.

Adopt local body language : Observing how people behave in the target environment can help you adopt appropriate body language. Consider gestures, postures, and facial expressions typical of the local culture.

Avoid distinguishing marks: Make sure you don't wear objects or clothing that could reveal your true identity. Remove jewelry or accessories that might attract attention.

Basic knowledge of culture: If you dress up to blend in with a foreign culture, familiarize yourself with some basic customs and social rules. This will prevent you from making mistakes that could betray your identity.

Behave like a local: Once you're dressed up, act like a local person. Follow local customs, interact with other people in a natural way, and avoid any behavior that might make you notice.

Be discreet: When you are in the field, be discreet in your movements and interactions. Avoid dwelling on a single place for too long and remain attentive to your surroundings.

Adapt to changes: Stay flexible and adapt quickly to changes in your environment. If necessary, adjust your disguise or behavior to suit the circumstances.

By following these tips, you will be able to blend into a specific environment by using the disguise in an effective and discreet way. Keep in mind that the success of this approach depends on preparation, careful observation and the ability to act in a natural and culturally appropriate way.

20. Using "Priming": Ask preliminary questions to prepare a source to provide more sensitive information.

At the heart of advanced intelligence techniques, priming is emerging as a powerful but subtle tool to prepare the ground before gathering sensitive information from sources. This strategic approach involves asking carefully designed preliminary questions to subconsciously influence how the source will respond to more critical questions. Let's dive into the mysteries of this clever method that allows intelligence professionals to access otherwise inaccessible information.

Priming is based on a well-established psychological reality: prior experiences and stimuli can influence our behavior, beliefs and responses. By asking preliminary questions, intelligence officers establish a favorable context that subtly conditions how the source will perceive and deal with subsequent issues.

One of the keys to priming is the skillful formulation of preliminary questions. Agents should create questions that evoke specific emotions, associations of ideas, or thought patterns. For example, by asking a question about positive memories related to a given location, the agent can cause the source to feel more inclined to cooperate and share more intimate information afterwards.

Psychological preparation is essential to create effective priming. Intelligence officers must understand human psychology and be attentive to the reactions of the source during the interaction. Poorly designed "Priming" can be detected by the source and fail to produce the expected results.

Priming can be used in different intelligence situations. During an interrogation, for example, the agent may start with innocuous questions on unimportant topics to establish a connection with the source and build trust. Then he can move on to more sensitive issues and get crucial information more easily through psychological preparation.

In the recruitment of informants, "Priming" can be used to arouse interest and motivation in a potential person. By asking questions about their skills, opinions or values, the agent can create a sense of belonging and encourage the person to collaborate more.

Priming can also be used in criminal investigations to influence the memory of a witness or victim. By asking preliminary questions about specific details of an event, the agent can subtly guide how the person remembers events and get more accurate information. By asking skillfully crafted preliminary questions, intelligence officers can set the stage and subtly influence the source's answers. However, this approach must be used with caution, transparency and respect for ethical principles to avoid abuse or manipulation. Priming remains a valuable tool for accessing crucial information and expanding intelligence horizons.

21. Travel Information Collection: Review travel itineraries, hotel reservations, etc., to trace a person's movements.

The collection of travel information often begins with the careful analysis of documents relating to the target's movements. Intelligence professionals study airline tickets, hotel reservations, itineraries, visa details, and other evidence to piece together the targeted person's past and future travel. This information can reveal clues about its activities, connections, and intentions.

Credit cards and bank statements can also be valuable sources of travel information. Intelligence officers scan these documents for travel-related expenses, airline ticket purchases, hotel reservations and other transactions that may reveal important details.

In addition to official documents, social networks play a vital role in collecting travel information. Photos, location statuses, and messages posted by the target or their contacts can provide valuable insights into their whereabouts and activities. Intelligence professionals use this information to discreetly track the target's movements and establish links with other sources of information.

The analysis of travel data can also be complemented by field surveys. Intelligence agents may interview witnesses, hotel employees, taxi drivers, and others involved in the target's movements to obtain additional information. These discrete surveys validate information gathered from documents and online sources.

The collection of travel information is a multidimensional technique that requires a methodical and meticulous approach. Intelligence professionals need to be on the lookout for every detail and use different sources to get a complete picture of the target's movements.

22. Search for conflicts of interest: Identify potential relationships that could influence the source to obtain biased information.

This clever approach involves identifying potential relationships from a source that could bias their information and influence their judgment. Let's dive into the intricacies of this strategy that allows intelligence professionals to skillfully navigate the gray areas to obtain balanced and reliable information.

The search for conflicts of interest begins with a thorough analysis of the source's links and affiliations. Intelligence officers examine personal, professional, and financial relationships that might lead the source to favor certain interests or preserve specific alliances.

This may include business partnerships, political affiliations, family ties, or financial benefits that could compromise the neutrality of the source.

Once these relationships are identified, intelligence professionals assess their potential impact on the information provided by the source. They ask themselves key questions: Does the source have a personal interest in the topic at hand? Is it in contact with parties involved in the case? Could his political affiliations influence his statements? These considerations make it possible to understand the situation in its overall context and to shed light on possible biases.

At the same time, intelligence officers keep in mind that the mere existence of conflicts of interest does not automatically mean that the source is unreliable. Relationships and affiliations are often inevitable in the complex world of intelligence, and many sources can provide valuable information despite potential connections.

However, the search for conflicts of interest is essential to contextualize the information received and determine the credibility of the sources. It helps detect hidden motivations and identify sources that might have malicious intentions or particular goals.

When recruiting informants, finding conflicts of interest is a delicate process. Officers should understand the individual's potential incentives to collaborate and assess whether their personal interests could impair their commitment to the mission. However, this approach must be conducted with caution to avoid any harm or misjudgment towards trustworthy individuals.

The search for conflicts of interest is also subject to ethical and legal considerations. Intelligence professionals must respect the fundamental rights of sources and act within the framework of privacy and data protection laws. The collection and analysis of sensitive information must be carried out with integrity and respect for the privacy of the individuals concerned.

In conclusion, conflict of interest research is proving to be a valuable tool for assessing the reliability and neutrality of intelligence sources. By identifying affiliations and links that could bias the information provided, intelligence professionals skillfully navigate the grey areas to obtain balanced and reliable information.

23. Intelligence gathering in public places: Obtaining information discreetly by listening to or observing conversations in public places.

This stealthy approach allows intelligence professionals to exploit public places such as cafes, parks, shopping malls and public transport to glean information without arousing suspicion. Let's discover how these seasoned ears capture fragments of information that sometimes prove crucial in unravelling the threads of intelligence.

The collection of information in public places requires extreme discretion and vigilance. Intelligence agents must blend in and adopt a banal attitude so as not to attract attention. They must master the art of active listening, listening attentively to surrounding conversations without being noticed. Similarly, discreet observation of interactions between people can provide valuable clues without requiring direct contact.

In these public places, intelligence professionals may witness informal conversations or encounters between individuals who unknowingly leak sensitive information. These seemingly innocuous fragments of information can be essential to complete an investigative puzzle or confirm suspicions.

In addition, gathering intelligence in public places can also offer tactical advantages. Officers can, for example, locate target individuals, track their movements, or make connections to other potential sources, all without revealing their presence or intent.

However, this technique is not without its challenges. Gathering information in public places requires sustained attention and keen judgment in sorting relevant information from background noise. Conversations and interactions can be complex and confusing, making it difficult to identify crucial information.

In addition, intelligence professionals must be aware of the ethical limitations of this technique. Listening or observing in public places raises questions of privacy and fundamental rights. Agents must therefore act with integrity and restraint so as not to violate the rights of individuals and avoid any misuse of the information collected.

In addition, intelligence gathering in public places may face operational constraints, particularly in high-traffic locations where it may be difficult to distinguish individuals of interest from others.

24. Credibility assessment: Analyzes the reliability and veracity of information provided by a source by cross-referencing it with other sources and evidence.

When it comes to assessing a source's credibility in the field of intelligence, it is essential to take a methodical and thoughtful approach. Here is a practical guide to discern the true from the false:

Verify the source: The first step is to verify the identity and authenticity of the source. Intelligence professionals must ensure that the source is what it claims to be. This may include verification of identity, professional references, and any other information that could confirm the legitimacy of the source.

Examine motivations: Understanding the motivations of the source is essential to assess its credibility. Intelligence officers need to ask themselves questions such as: Why is the source providing this information? What are his personal interests? Are there any reasons why she might want to bias or distort the truth?

Analyze consistency: The information provided by the source should be consistent with other available sources and evidence. Intelligence professionals need to look for correlations and commonalities between information from different sources to verify its veracity.

Cross-referencing data: Cross-referencing information with other independent sources is an effective way to verify its accuracy. Intelligence officers need to seek converging information from different sources to strengthen their assessment.

Examine physical evidence: Physical evidence, such as official documents, recordings, images and additional testimony, are essential elements to support the information provided by the source. Intelligence professionals should look for hard evidence to confirm or deny the source's statements.

Assess past credibility: The past credibility of the source can be an important indicator of its reliability. Intelligence officers must seek a background of the source by examining its previous statements and their veracity.

Consider the big picture: Credibility assessment cannot be done in isolation. Intelligence professionals must consider the overall context of the information, including political, social, and economic conditions, to understand the potential motivations of the source and the factors that could influence its statements.

Remain vigilant: Credibility assessment is an ongoing and evolving process. Intelligence professionals must remain vigilant and question their findings as new information emerges.

In short, assessing the credibility of a source in the field of intelligence requires rigour, judgment and objectivity. By following these practical steps, intelligence professionals are better equipped to discern truth from falsehood and obtain reliable and valuable information for their mission. However, it is important to keep in mind that credibility assessment is a complex art that requires an informed and thoughtful approach to preserving intelligence integrity.

OSINT techniques

In today's digital age, sources of information are ubiquitous and accessible to all. Open source intelligence (OSINT) has become an increasingly popular intelligence discipline for professionals in a variety of fields, from national security services to corporations and investigative journalists. With its unlimited potential for information from public sources, OSINT is proving to be a goldmine for those who know how to exploit its resources.

The power of OSINT lies in its diversity. The information collected can come from sources as varied as traditional media, online publications, blogs, social networks, public databases, websites, government reports and official documents. This abundance of information opens up invaluable opportunities for those seeking intelligence on topics ranging from market trends to terrorist activities to social movements.

For investigative journalists, OSINT has become an essential tool for conducting their investigations. Through advanced online research techniques, they can collect crucial information to support their reporting. Senior journalists have used OSINT to trace corruption networks, uncover financial scandals, and uncover human rights violations. OSINT broadens the scope of their investigative work, offering unexpected leads and unexplored angles.

Similarly, in the area of national security and counter-terrorism, the OSINT plays a crucial role. Intelligence agencies use social media and websites to monitor the activities of terrorist groups, identify radicalized individuals, and anticipate potential threats. The OSINT analysis complements other sources of confidential information, providing a comprehensive and detailed picture of the security situation.

Companies have also found a goldmine in OSINT for competitive intelligence and informed decision-making. Analysis of market trends, competitor activities, and public reactions can be a deciding factor in a company's success or failure. Economic intelligence specialists use OSINT to gather strategic information, anticipate market movements and seize business opportunities.

The effectiveness of OSINT lies in its complementarity with other forms of intelligence, such as human intelligence (HUMINT), geospatial intelligence (GEOINT) and signal intelligence (SIGINT). The OSINT can corroborate and enrich the information obtained through these other means, thus providing a comprehensive and balanced view of complex situations.

However, the use of OSINT is not without its challenges and limitations. The abundance of information available can make collection tedious, requiring advanced research tools and skills. In addition, the reliability of the information found may vary, as OSINT does not guarantee the veracity of sources. Intelligence professionals must therefore exercise judgment and caution when using this information to make important decisions.

25. Search on conventional search engines (Google, Bing, etc.).

Conventional search engines, such as Google, Bing, and others, have become go-to tools for Open Source Intelligence (OSINT) in today's digital world. These search engines provide access to an impressive amount of public information online, making them essential resources for researchers, journalists, analysts and intelligence professionals.

Searching on conventional search engines offers several OSINT advantages. First of all, these search engines are easy to access and free for all users, making them widely accessible. In addition, their user-friendliness and ease of use make them suitable for users of all levels of computer skills. Finally, their ability to index a wide range of websites and online media provides a complete and varied overview of the information available.

When searching on conventional search engines, several techniques and strategies can be employed to optimize results and gather relevant information. Here are some tips and tricks for an effective search:

Use advanced search operators: Conventional search engines offer a series of advanced search operators that filter results and narrow searches. Operators such as quotation marks for exact phrases, Boolean operators for combining keywords, and date range operators are particularly useful for targeting specific information.

Explore related search results : Conventional search engines often display related search results at the bottom of the page, which can provide additional leads for the search. By clicking on these links, users can discover related sources of information and expand their search scope.

Use relevant keywords: Selecting relevant keywords is essential to get accurate search results. Keywords must be specific and relevant to the subject of the search. The use of synonyms and related terms can also broaden search results.

Explore different types of results: Conventional search engines display a variety of results, such as websites, images, videos, news, and many more. Exploring different types of results can provide complementary information and varied perspectives on the topic being sought.

Check sources: When searching on conventional search engines, it is essential to check the credibility and reliability of the sources found. Reviewing the reputation of the website and verifying information from multiple sources can help ensure the accuracy of the data.

Use specialized search tools: In addition to conventional search engines, there are specialized search tools for OSINT that allow you to refine results and access specific databases. These tools can be particularly useful for targeted research in specific areas.

It is important to note that searching on conventional search engines also has limitations when it comes to OSINT. First, some information may not be indexed or publicly accessible, which may limit the scope of the search. In addition, research on conventional search engines is often limited to content available online, leaving out offline and confidential information.

Searching on conventional search engines is an essential pillar of Open Source Intelligence. These publicly accessible tools offer a wealth of public information online, which can be used for surveys, analysis, reports and many other applications. By judiciously exploiting advanced search operators, selecting relevant keywords and checking the credibility of sources, OSINT professionals can take full advantage of the wealth of information available on these search engines to inform their work and make informed decisions.

26. Advanced search with Boolean operators (AND, OR, NOT) to refine results.

Advanced search with Boolean operators (AND, OR, NOT) is an essential skill for Open Source Intelligence professionals. These operators make it possible to combine keywords and filter search results accurately, which helps to obtain relevant information and refine the results. Here's how to effectively use these operators to maximize advanced OSINT search:

The "AND" operator: The "AND" operator is used to search for documents that contain two specific keywords, by combining them. For example, typing "cybersecurity AND attacks", the results will only show pages that contain both the words "cybersecurity" and "attacks". This makes it possible to target specific information and refine the search.

The "OR" operator: The "OR" operator is used to search for documents that contain any of the specified keywords. For example, typing "cybersecurity OR computer security", the results will include pages that contain either the word "cybersecurity" or the word "computer security". This broadens the scope of the search and makes it possible to find information related to related topics.

The "NOT" operator: The "NOT" operator is used to exclude specific keywords from search results. For example, typing "NOT bitcoin cryptocurrencies" will not include pages that contain the word "bitcoin". This helps eliminate irrelevant information and focus on specific topics.

Parentheses for group logic: By using parentheses, it is possible to combine multiple Boolean operators to create complex search logic. For example, typing "(artificial intelligence OR AI) AND (applications OR uses)", the results will show pages that contain either the terms "artificial intelligence" or "AI", as well as the terms "applications" or "uses". This makes it possible to further refine the search and obtain specific information.

Using quotation marks for exact expressions: To find an exact expression, quotation marks can be used. For example, when typing "artificial intelligence", the results will only include pages that contain the exact phrase "artificial intelligence", not pages that contain the separate words "intelligence" and "artificial".

Combine multiple operators for complex searches: By combining Boolean operators with relevant keywords, quotation marks for exact expressions, and parentheses for group logic, OSINT researchers can perform complex and targeted searches. This approach makes it possible to obtain accurate and relevant results for specific topics.

Advanced search with Boolean operators is an essential skill for OSINT and intelligence professionals. By using the "AND" operator to combine specific keywords, the "OR" operator to search for related terms, the "NOT" operator to exclude irrelevant keywords, and by using quotation marks for exact phrases, researchers can refine their searches and obtain relevant and accurate information. By combining these techniques with advanced online research skills, professionals can maximize their efficiency and productivity in gathering information from open sources.

27. Using OSINT-specific search engines (e.g. Shodan, Censys) to find information on Internet-connected devices.

Using OSINT-specific search engines, such as Shodan and Censys, is a common and powerful practice for finding information on internet-connected devices. These specialized search engines are designed to scan the web for devices, servers, and other equipment accessible online, providing a single view of the Internet of Things (IoT) and network infrastructure.

Shodan: Shodan is often referred to as the "search engine for connected objects". It crawls and indexes devices that use communication protocols such as HTTP, FTP, SSH, SNMP, as well as devices without authentication, making some information potentially available to the general public. Shodan's results can provide detailed information about devices such as security cameras, routers, industrial automation systems, and much more. Security researchers, network professionals, and OSINT professionals use Shodan to identify vulnerable or misconfigured devices, which can be critical for information security and protection.

Censys: Censys is another OSINT search engine that focuses on discovering and analyzing Internet-connected networks and devices. Censys also indexes SSL/TLS certificates, domain names, IP addresses, and specific protocols, allowing researchers to collect information about servers, websites, and other online services. Censys results can be useful for assessing the security and compliance of online infrastructures.

Keyword and filter search: These OSINT-specific search engines offer advanced keyword search and filtering capabilities, allowing searchers to specifically target the information they are looking for. Researchers can use specific keywords to identify particular devices, software, or services, and apply filters to refine the results based on the needs of their survey.

Identifying vulnerabilities and security issues: The results of these search engines can sometimes reveal sensitive information, such as devices that are misconfigured or have security vulnerabilities. This can be a valuable resource for security researchers and risk management professionals, as they can use this information to alert affected device owners and improve the overall security of connected infrastructures.

In conclusion, the use of OSINT-specific search engines such as Shodan and Censys offers unique opportunities to explore the Internet of Things and network infrastructures. OSINT professionals, security researchers, and analysts can leverage these tools to discover connected devices, assess their security and configuration, and identify potential vulnerabilities. However, it is paramount to use these tools responsibly, respecting the privacy of users and complying with applicable laws and regulations.

28. Browse web archives and cached pages to find deleted information.

Browsing web archives and cached pages is a valuable technique for finding deleted or old information on the Internet. Web archives and caches are essential resources for researchers, journalists, and investigators looking to recover valuable information that might otherwise be lost.

Web Archive: Web archives are online information libraries that record snapshots of web pages at different points in time. Organizations such as the Internet Archive (archive.org) are dedicated to preserving web pages and their content. These archives can be searched for previous versions of websites, archived news articles, blogs, and other information that may have been modified or deleted over time.

Search engine cached pages : When search engines index web pages, they often save cached copies of those pages. These cached copies can be accessed to access previous versions of websites, even after the original pages have been deleted or modified. By using the advanced search features of search engines, it is possible to find archived versions of specific pages.

Using the "wayback machine" tool: The Internet Archive offers a tool called "Wayback Machine", which allows users to browse archived snapshots of websites. By entering the URL of a website into this tool, researchers can go back in time to view previous versions of that site. This can be especially useful for finding lost or deleted information.

Keyword search : To effectively use web archives and cached pages, it is important to formulate specific and relevant search queries. Researchers can use specific keywords, domain names, or article titles to find specific information in the archive.

Verifying the accuracy of information: When using web archives and cached pages, it is essential to carefully verify the accuracy and authenticity of the retrieved information. Because these resources may contain archived versions of modified or deleted pages, it is important to cross-reference the information with other sources to ensure its reliability.

Privacy and copyright: The use of web archives and cached pages must be done in a manner that respects the copyright and privacy of the website owners. It is important to comply with applicable laws and regulations regarding the use of archived online content.

In conclusion, browsing web archives and cached pages is a powerful OSINT technique for finding deleted or old information on the Internet. Web archives and search engine caches provide valuable access to previous versions of websites, news articles, and other online content that can be of great use to researchers and investigators. However, it is essential to use these resources carefully and verify the accuracy of the information retrieved to ensure the reliability of the search results.

29. Search for information about WHOIS domains to discover website owners.

Searching for information about WHOIS domains is a common practice in Open Source Intelligence (OSINT) to discover website owners and obtain important information about domain names. The WHOIS system is a public database that records the contact information of domain name owners, hosting providers, and network administrators. Here's how this technique is used in a practical way:

Access WHOIS databases: There are many websites and online tools that allow users to access WHOIS databases. These tools are generally easy to use and freely accessible. Some hosting providers also offer WHOIS lookups directly on their sites.

Domain name search: To get information about a specific domain, simply enter the domain name in the WHOIS tool of your choice. The information provided may include the domain owner's name, contact information, hosting provider, domain creation date, expiration date, associated name servers, and other technical details.

Use of information for surveys: Information obtained from WHOIS lookup can be used for in-depth OSINT surveys. For example, knowing the owner of a website can be useful for identifying the author of a blog or news site, investigating cases of online fraud or abuse, or tracking the activities of a suspicious site.

Compliance with data protection policies: It is important to note that some WHOIS information may be subject to data protection policies, such as the European Union's General Data Protection Regulation (GDPR). As a result, some personal information of domain owners may be hidden or made inaccessible in public WHOIS databases.

Using advanced search tools: Some advanced WHOIS tools offer additional features, such as searching by IP address ranges, searching for domains associated with the same entity, or checking for recent changes in WHOIS records. These features can be useful for conducting more in-depth research and identifying relationships between different domains.

30. Analysis of email headers to get information about the sender and email provider.

Email header analysis is an open source intelligence (OSINT) technique used to obtain information about the sender and email provider of a given email. Email headers contain important technical information about the message path, the servers involved, and the various stages of transmission. Here's how this technique is used in a practical way:

Access to email headers: To access email headers, it is usually sufficient to open the email in the email client used. The procedure for viewing headers varies depending on the email client, but it is usually possible to access this information by looking for options such as "Show full header" or "Message header".

Header analysis: Once email headers are displayed, researchers can analyze the information they contain. Headers can include details such as the IP address of the sending server, the IP address of the receiving server, the message transmission path, the name of the email provider used, and other technical information.

Using header analysis tools: There are online tools that allow users to automatically scan email headers to get detailed information about the sender and email provider. These tools can provide additional information such as the approximate geographical location of the sender and the potential authenticity of the email.

Origin IP Address Identification : The IP address of the sending server in email headers can be used to identify the approximate geographic location of the sender. This can be useful for detecting suspicious activity or phishing attempts from certain parts of the world.

Authenticity verification: Email header scanning can also be used to verify the authenticity of emails, detecting attempts to "spoofing" or falsify the sender's address. This can be especially important when fighting phishing and other forms of security attacks.

Email header analysis is a valuable OSINT technique that can obtain information about the sender and email provider of a given email. This technique can be used to verify the authenticity of emails, detect phishing attempts and other suspicious activity, as well as identify the approximate geographical location of the sender.

31. Using reverse image search to identify the origin or use of certain images.

The use of reverse image search is a technique that identifies the origin or use of certain images online. This method is particularly useful when you want to verify the authenticity of an image, trace the source of an image, or find out if an image has been used elsewhere on the Internet. Here's how this technique works and how it's used in a practical way:

How reverse image search works: Reverse image search works by uploading a specific image to a specialized search engine or pasting the image URL. The search engine then searches its database to find similar or identical visual matches. The results display where the image was found on the web, the sites that use it, and possibly information about its origin.

Using reverse image search tools: There are several free online tools that allow you to perform a reverse image search. Among the best known are Google Images, TinEye, Bing Visual Search, Yandex Images, etc. Each tool may have its own strengths and limitations in terms of index coverage and accuracy of results.

Image authenticity verification : Reverse image search is often used to verify whether a given image is authentic or has been altered or manipulated. By comparing the original image with the search results, significant variations or differences can be detected.

Discovering the source of an image: When an image is found in reverse image search results, it can be used to discover the original source or author of the image. This can be useful to properly assign credit to the author or to get information about the context in which the image was taken.

Searching for image usage: Reverse image search is also used to find out if an image has been used elsewhere on the Internet. This can be particularly useful for finding images that have been stolen or used without permission.

Privacy and copyright: When using reverse image search, it is important to respect the privacy of data subjects and comply with copyright laws and regulations. The use of certain images may be subject to legal or ethical restrictions.

In conclusion, reverse image search is a powerful technique that can identify the origin or use of certain images online. This method can be used to verify the authenticity of images, discover their original source, and find their use on the Internet.

32. Collecting metadata from media files (photos, videos) to get hidden information.

To collect metadata from media files, here are the concrete steps to follow and the information you can find:

Using metadata extraction software: Start by downloading metadata extraction software specifically designed for media files. There are many free and paid options available online. Some popular software includes ExifTool, Metashield Analyzer, and Adobe Photoshop (for images). Install the software on your computer or device.

Select media file: Open the software and select the media file from which you want to extract metadata. Make sure you choose the original file, as metadata can be edited or deleted when an image is compressed or edited.

Extract metadata: When you have selected the file, start the process of extracting metadata from the software. This will scan the file and display the information available in the metadata.

Information available in metadata: The information you can find in metadata varies depending on the type of media file. For images, metadata can include the date and time of shooting, the geographic coordinates (latitude and longitude) where the photo was taken, the model of the camera used, camera settings (shutter speed, aperture, ISO sensitivity, etc.), and sometimes even the name of the author or photographer. For videos, metadata can contain information about video resolution, codec used, video duration, etc.

Analyze metadata: Once you have extracted the metadata, carefully analyze the available information. Check the date and time of shooting to make sure the image or video is authentic. Geographic coordinates can be useful for tracing the location where the file was captured. Details about the camera or video camera can give indications of the quality of the file.

Using metadata extraction software, you can access details such as shooting date and time, geographic coordinates, camera settings, and many more. This information can be useful for verifying the authenticity of files, tracing their origin or creator, and uncovering additional information that may be relevant in investigations and research. However, it is important to comply with privacy and data protection policies when using this technique to respect the privacy of data subjects.

33. Social media monitoring to find personal or business information.

Social media monitoring has become an essential tool for investigators, researchers and professionals. With billions of active users on various platforms, social media offers a wealth of publicly available personal and business information. This technique allows you to get details about people, their habits, their connections and much more. However, its use also raises questions about privacy and ethics, requiring a balance between collecting information and respecting individual rights.

The first step in social media monitoring is to identify relevant platforms. Facebook, Twitter, LinkedIn, Instagram, YouTube, and others are among the most popular platforms. Each platform offers a range of different information, from holiday photos to professional achievements. This diversity allows investigators to get a more complete overview of their subject.

Once the platforms have been identified, the search for relevant profiles is crucial. Conventional search engines, as well as advanced tools, help to find the profiles of the people concerned. Boolean operators (AND, OR, NOT) refine the results for more precise targeting.

Each social media profile contains a treasure trove of personal and professional information. Names, email addresses, phone numbers, places of residence, jobs, interests, and much more are publicly available. On LinkedIn, for example, professional skills, achievements, and professional connections are available. Careful analysis of this information can provide essential clues for investigations.

Social media monitoring is not a one-time activity. Users regularly update their profiles, post new information, and interact with other users. Continuous monitoring allows you to gather up-to-date information and track developments.

For effective monitoring, monitoring tools specifically designed for social media are available. These tools organize monitored profiles, send notifications for important updates, and help OSINT professionals collect information more efficiently.

Social media monitoring is a powerful tool for collecting personal and professional information. Social media monitoring offers immense potential, but it is up to everyone to ensure that its use is done in a way that respects individual rights.

34. Search for geolocated data (geolocation) to identify specific places.

Geolocation data searching, also known as geolocation, is a technique that involves using location-based information to identify specific locations. This approach makes it possible to discover specific places where events have occurred, individuals have visited, or activities have taken place. Here's how this technique can be used:

Use of geotag data: Many photos and videos posted on social media and other online platforms include geolocation data in their metadata. Geotag information can be used to trace the locations where media was captured, which can be valuable in determining a person's movements or the location of a specific event.

Location tag analysis: Social networks such as Instagram allow users to add location tags to their posts. By searching for specific location tags, investigators can gain information about places frequented by a person or places associated with a particular event.

Check-in data mining: Some apps and social networks allow users to report their presence in a location by performing a "check-in". Examining this check-in data can reveal places frequented by a person or popular places for specific activities.

Location history analysis: Mobile devices and online services often record users' location history. Investigators can obtain location history data from service providers or by examining the location settings of the devices themselves. This information can help reconstruct a person's movements over a period of time.

Search online mapping services: Online mapping services such as Google Maps can provide information about specific places, addresses, businesses, tourist attractions, etc. Using these services, investigators can obtain detailed information about places of interest.

Sensor data analysis: Some devices, such as smartphones and wearables, may collect location-related sensor data, such as GPS or Wi-Fi data. Analyzing this data can help identify a person's movements and movement patterns.

Mining government public data: In some countries, governments make available public geospatial databases that contain information on specific locations, borders, infrastructure, etc. These sources can be used to obtain more official location-based information.

In conclusion, geolocation data search is a powerful technique that can identify specific locations using location-based information. By combining various sources of information, investigators can trace a person's movements, uncover places of interest, and obtain valuable clues for their investigations and searches.

35. Scan public Wi-Fi networks to get information about frequented locations.

Public Wi-Fi network analysis is an open source intelligence (OSINT) technique that provides information about locations frequented by individuals or groups. Public Wi-Fi networks are commonly available in public places such as cafes, restaurants, airports, hotels, and other public spaces. Here's how this technique can be used:

Reading Wi-Fi Network Names (SSIDs): By scanning available Wi-Fi networks in a specific geographic area, it is possible to read network names (SSIDs) broadcast by public Wi-Fi access points. Some users choose personal or location-specific network names, which can reveal information about the locations frequented by individuals.

Recurring connection location analysis: By monitoring recurring connections to public Wi-Fi networks, it is possible to identify locations frequently visited by an individual or group. For example, if a person regularly connects to a Wi-Fi network at a specific coffee shop every morning, it may indicate a favorite or work location.

Collection of access point information: Public Wi-Fi hotspots can be geolocated, meaning they are associated with specific GPS coordinates. By collecting this information across multiple access points, investigators can map the locations of public Wi-Fi networks in a given area and determine places of interest.

Identification of popular places: By analyzing public Wi-Fi hotspots that attract a large number of connections, it is possible to identify popular places such as shopping malls, train stations, parks, etc.

Analysis of connection times: By examining connection times to public Wi-Fi networks, investigators can obtain information about a person's travel habits. For example, frequent connections to access points in different neighborhoods or cities may indicate regular travel.

Association with specific locations: Some businesses and organizations use specifically named public Wi-Fi networks to identify their locations. For example, a Wi-Fi network named "XYZ Cafe" can be associated with a specific coffee shop. By collecting and analyzing this information, investigators can uncover specific locations.

It is important to note that analyzing public Wi-Fi networks raises questions of privacy and ethics. The information collected must be used in a lawful and ethical manner, complying with privacy and data protection laws and regulations. In addition, this technique is often subject to technical and legal limitations, as access to and use of public Wi-Fi networks may be restricted in some countries or regions.

36. Search forums and online groups to find relevant discussions.

Searching forums and online groups is an Open Source Intelligence (OSINT) technique that makes it possible to find relevant discussions on specific topics. Online forums, discussion groups and social media platforms are spaces where people exchange information, share opinions and discuss various topics. Here's how this technique can be used:

Identification of relevant forums and groups: To begin with, it is important to identify online forums and groups that are relevant to the research topic. These forums can specialize in specific areas, such as technology, health, travel, etc. Social media platforms like Reddit, Facebook, and LinkedIn also host discussion groups on various topics.

Use of relevant keywords: To perform an effective search, it is essential to use relevant keywords related to the search topic. These keywords can include product names, personal names, technical terms, etc. Using specific keywords, investigators can target discussions that are directly related to their topic.

Analysis of discussions: Once relevant forums and groups have been identified, it is time to analyze the discussions taking place there. Investigators may search for specific topics, questions, opinions, complaints, praise, etc. This analysis provides useful insights into user opinions, trends, emerging issues, and much more.

Cross-referencing information: To validate the information found, it is important to cross-check the data with other sources. For example, if a forum mentions a new product, it is a good idea to check the information with the manufacturer or official resellers. Cross-checking information helps to ensure the reliability of sources.

Comment analysis: User feedback can be a treasure trove of information. The opinions, personal experiences, complaints, and praise shared in the comments can provide valuable clues about the products, services, or events in question.

Ongoing monitoring: Online discussions are constantly evolving. Investigators should therefore conduct ongoing monitoring of relevant forums and groups to stay informed of updates, new discussions and developments on the topic.

It is essential to remember that online forums and groups are public spaces where users share their opinions freely. However, investigators must respect the rules and policies of each forum or group, as well as the individual rights and privacy of users.

37. Data leak search to identify information exposed online.

Data leak searching, also known as data leak search, is a technique that aims to identify confidential or sensitive information that has been exposed online as a result of security incidents or data breaches. Data leaks can include information such as login credentials, passwords, personal information, financial data, trade secrets, and much more. Here's how this technique can be used:

Monitoring compromised data sources: For starters, investigators need to monitor compromised data sources that are often shared on underground forums, hacking sites, encrypted messaging channels, and even social networks. These sources may contain stolen databases or data files that have been made public.

Use of specialized search tools: There are specialized tools designed to search for and analyze data leaks online. These tools can help identify exposed data by searching for specific keywords, domain names, email addresses, and more.

Verification of leak sources: It is important to verify the credibility and authenticity of leak sources. Some sources may be hoaxes or attempts at misinformation. By verifying the provenance and quality of the data exposed, investigators can ensure the reliability of the information.

Analysis of exposed data: Once leak data has been identified, it is essential to analyze it to understand the nature and extent of exposure. Investigators can search for sensitive information, identify the individuals or organizations involved, and assess potential security and privacy risks.

Notification of relevant parties: If sensitive information about individuals or organizations is discovered in data breaches, it is important to notify them so that they can take appropriate measures to protect their data and enhance its security.

Preventing future leaks: Scanning for data leaks can also help identify security holes or vulnerabilities that led to information exposure. By understanding the causes of leaks, organizations can take steps to strengthen their security and prevent future data breaches.

It is crucial to stress that data leak detection must be carried out in compliance with data protection and privacy laws and regulations. Investigators must also be aware of the potential risks associated with accessing and handling sensitive data, and must act ethically and responsibly throughout the process.

38. Using Google dorks to find sensitive documents and information.

Using Google dorks is an advanced open source intelligence (OSINT) technique that involves using specific search operators in the Google search engine to find sensitive documents and information that are not normally accessible via conventional searches. Google dorks allow investigators to refine their searches to target specific information and access content that is not indexed in traditional search results. Here's how this technique can be used:

Understanding search operators: Google dorks are combinations of search operators, such as "site:", "filetype:", "intitle:", "inurl:", "cache:", etc. Each operator has a specific function that allows you to filter search results based on specific criteria.

Search for sensitive documents: Investigators can use Google dorks to search for sensitive documents such as financial reports, databases, confidential documents, files containing personal information, and much more. For example, using "filetype:pdf" or "filetype:xls" in the search, they can find PDF or Excel files that contain relevant information.

Search login pages: Google dorks can also be used to find insecure login pages or admin pages that could be vulnerable to hacking attacks. This can allow investigators to report security vulnerabilities to the owners of the affected site.

Search for exposed data: Using Google dorks, investigators can search for potentially exposed information online, such as email addresses, phone numbers, passwords, IP addresses, and more. This can help them assess security risks to the individuals or organizations involved.

Verification of results: As with any OSINT search, it is essential to check the credibility and authenticity of the results obtained from Google dorks. Some information may be outdated, incorrect or from unreliable sources.

It is important to point out that the use of Google dorks raises ethical and legal questions. Some information accessible through Google Dorks may be confidential and unauthorized access to it may be considered illegal. Investigators must act responsibly and ethically, respecting applicable data protection and privacy laws and rules.

39. Crawl file-sharing sites (e.g., Dropbox, Google Drive) to find exposed data.

File sharing site crawling is a technique that makes it possible to find data exposed online on popular file storage and sharing platforms such as Dropbox, Google Drive, OneDrive, etc. These platforms allow users to store and share files online, but some information may be made public or accessed by mistake. Here's how this technique can be used:

Finding public links: Users of file-sharing sites can create public links to share files with others. These public links can be indexed by search engines, which means that data can be found by performing a targeted search with specific keywords.

Using search operators: Just like Google dorks, specific search operators can be used to filter search results on file-sharing platforms. For example, terms such as "site:dropbox.com" or "site:drive.google.com" can be used to specifically target files hosted on these platforms.

Checking access permissions: Some data may be exposed due to poor security configurations or human error. Investigators should check file access permissions to ensure they can legitimately access the data. Unauthorized access to private files can be illegal and a violation of privacy.

Metadata analysis: File metadata can contain valuable information such as author name, creation date, changes made, etc. This metadata can be useful for understanding the origin and authenticity of files.

Owner notification: If sensitive data is found exposed online, it is essential to notify the owners of the files or the administrators of the platforms concerned so that they can take appropriate measures to secure their data.

It is important to note that searching for exposed data on file-sharing sites must be done ethically and responsibly. Investigators must respect copyright, intellectual property and data confidentiality. Unauthorized access to private files may be illegal and result in legal consequences.

40. Search for usernames and nicknames on different sites to link online profiles.

The search for usernames and pseudonyms on different sites is one that aims to link a person's online profiles from the different usernames or pseudonyms they use on the Internet. This technique is often used to gather information about a person, to understand their online behavior, interests, affiliations, and possibly identify potential security or reputational risks. Here's how this technique can be implemented:

Collection of known usernames and aliases: The first step is to collect all known usernames or pseudonyms of a person. This information can be found on social media profiles, forums, personal websites, or other online sources where the person has publicly used these identifiers.

Social media research: Social media is one of the main areas where people use usernames or pseudonyms to interact. Using known usernames or pseudonyms, investigators can search social networking sites such as Facebook, Twitter, LinkedIn, Instagram, etc., to find matching profiles.

Forum and blog search: Forums and blogs are other places where people often use usernames or pseudonyms to participate in discussions. Investigators can use specialized search engines to search for these usernames on relevant forums and blogs.

Online gaming platform research: Online gaming platforms are popular for users who create accounts with pseudonyms to play and interact with other players. Investigators can search for these pseudonyms on online gaming platforms to find related profiles.

Search personal websites or blogs: Some people may have personal websites or blogs where they use a specific username. Investigators can search for these usernames on search engines to find links to these websites.

Analysis of online activities: Once online profiles linked to usernames or pseudonyms are found, investigators can analyze the person's online activities. This can include social media posts, forum comments, blog posts, shared photos and videos, etc. This analysis can help to understand the person's interests, affiliations, and behavior online.

41. Search for phone numbers to identify owners or associated locations.

This technique is used in various scenarios, such as searching for personal information, identifying phone spammers, or locating unknown numbers. Here's how to conduct a phone number lookup using OSINT:

Reverse lookup in online phone books: Online phone directories such as White Pages or Yellow Pages are useful sources for finding a phone number and identifying the associated owner. You can enter the phone number in the search field and view the results for information about the owner, including name and address.

Use of search engines: Search engines such as Google can also be used to search for a phone number. You can enter the number in quotation marks in the search bar to get specific results related to that number. Sometimes additional information, such as social media profiles or company listings, may appear in the results.

Social Media Search: If you're looking for information about a particular phone number, it's a good idea to check social media. Some users associate their phone number with their social profiles, which can provide additional information about the owner.

Using number finder apps: There are apps and websites specifically designed to look up phone numbers and provide information about associated owners. Some apps even allow you to block or report spam numbers.

Searching public databases for phone numbers: Some organizations and businesses publish lists of phone numbers for a variety of reasons. It may be useful to consult these databases to identify specific numbers.

Search forums and discussion sites: Sometimes phone numbers are shared on forums or chat sites. By conducting targeted searches on these platforms, you could find information about the number you are looking for.

Use of specialized OSINT tools: There are specialized OSINT tools and software that can be used to search for phone numbers and obtain owner information. These tools can automate the search process and provide more complete results.

It is important to note that the search for telephone numbers under OSINT must be done ethically and legally. It is essential to respect privacy and applicable laws regarding the collection of personal information. Phone number lookup should be used for legitimate purposes, such as searching for public information or protecting against unwanted calls.

Source manipulation techniques

Behind the scenes of the intelligence world, where secrets overlap and information is as much a weapon as a shield, a set of skills well known to insiders emerges: "Source Manipulation Techniques". While OSINT (Open Source Intelligence) aims to collect information that is open and accessible to all, offensive intelligence deploys a variety of underhand tactics to control information and shape narrative for strategic purposes.

In this crucial chapter of our exploration of the mysteries of offensive intelligence, we will dive into the heart of an insidious dimension of modern espionage. From intelligence agencies to interest groups to companies eager to know the weaknesses of their competitors, all seek to manipulate information sources to better influence the decisions and perceptions of their targets.

Like a maestro conducting his orchestra, source manipulators deploy sophisticated strategies to sow doubt, create illusions and conceal their true intentions. From the subtle "Priming" to shape the answers, to the decoys carefully designed to trap their opponents, every note in this symphony of manipulation aims to dictate the direction of information and control the game of appearances.

Readers will discover the set of psychological tactics used to gain unconscious buy-in, the methods of disinformation cleverly orchestrated to sow confusion, and the countermeasure strategies to thwart attempts at manipulation. We will also dive into the intricacies of collecting sensitive and confidential sources, where issues mingle with risks, and where the quest for relevant information can turn into a dangerous dance.

In this universe where words and silences are weapons, we must keep in mind that the manipulation of sources is a double-edged sword. If it can serve the interests of the one who wields this weapon with skill, it can also turn against him, revealing flaws and weakening his position.

It is crucial to remember that the search for truth must always remain at the heart of engagement in offensive intelligence. By revealing the techniques of manipulation of sources, we wish to enlighten intelligence actors on the ethical issues surrounding this practice, and to make them aware of the importance of integrity in the collection and analysis of information.

So, go behind the scenes of the world of offensive intelligence and explore with us the well-kept secrets of "Source Manipulation Techniques". In this quest to understand how information can be a powerful tool for control, let us keep in mind that in a complex and interconnected world, vigilance and critical thinking are the best bulwarks against attempts at manipulation.

42. Active listening: Be attentive and receptive to information provided by clients and sources.

Active listening, like listening in the hustle and bustle of information, is an essential skill for any intelligence professional, investigator, private investigator or business intelligence consultant. At the heart of this technique is caring curiosity and empathy, which help to understand the needs and motivations of customers, as well as the intentions and emotions of sources.

In the art of active listening, silence is golden. Listening without interruption, without judgment, and without prejudice, allows to offer a space of trust conducive to communication. Establishing an authentic connection with interlocutors encourages them to engage sincerely, revealing valuable information that might otherwise remain buried.

The key to active listening is the ability to ask the right questions, dig deeper when necessary, and rephrase information to ensure mutual understanding. It is not just a matter of hearing the words, but of deciphering the emotions and the unspoken, which can sometimes reveal more than what is expressed explicitly.

In the context of intelligence, active listening is all the more crucial during interrogations, confidential interviews, or interactions with potential sources. The nuances of nonverbal communication, such as gestures, facial expressions, and intonations, can reveal key information for understanding the intentions and credibility of the interlocutors.

Active listening is not a passive skill, but rather an act of conscious presence. It means being totally immersed in the present moment, giving your full attention to the other person. By taking this approach, intelligence professionals can gather important details, subtle clues, and crucial nuances that help build a more complete picture of the situation.

It is also essential to cultivate an open-minded attitude, avoiding prejudices and hasty conclusions. Each source or customer is unique, and their experiences and perspectives can differ significantly. By remaining open to all possibilities, we broaden the horizons of information, while avoiding falling into the trap of stereotypes or cognitive biases.

Ultimately, active listening is a powerful tool for gathering information and developing trusting relationships. It enables intelligence professionals to build strong bridges with their clients and sources, while ensuring richer, more accurate, and more comprehensive information gathering.

In today's context where information is ubiquitous, but often scattered and disorganized, active listening emerges as an invaluable skill to unravel the threads of truth and reality. Through this approach, intelligence professionals can rise above the noise of information and access the quintessential knowledge needed to accomplish their mission ethically, honestly, and effectively.

43. Empathy: Understanding and sharing the feelings and emotions of others.

Empathy, like a lantern illuminating the darkest recesses of the human soul, is a fundamental quality for any intelligence professional. It goes far beyond active listening by allowing you to truly feel and understand the emotions, motivations and experiences of others.

At the heart of empathy is the ability to put oneself in the other's shoes, to perceive one's emotions and to share one's experience. It is a kind of emotional bridge that connects the intelligence professional to his clients, his sources, and even his targets. By connecting to their inner reality, it becomes possible to grasp hidden nuances, emotional subtleties, and emotional clues that would otherwise escape superficial analysis.

In the intelligence context, empathy is paramount when interacting with sensitive or vulnerable sources. Understanding their fears, wants, motivations and needs is essential to building trust and cooperation. By expressing sincere empathy, intelligence professionals show their interlocutors that they are heard, respected and taken into account.

Empathy is also a valuable tool for decoding the behaviors and emotional reactions of interviewees or observers. Emotions can be indicative of hidden truths, lies, fears, or underlying motivations. By immersing themselves in the feelings of the other, the intelligence professional is better able to decipher these subtle signals and make informed decisions.

However, it is important to note that empathy should not be confused with sympathy. Sympathy involves feeling the emotions of the other with compassion, while empathy is a more neutral quality, which consists of understanding emotions without judging them. Keeping an emotional distance while being receptive to the emotions of the other is essential to preserve the clarity of thought and objectivity necessary in the intelligence world.

44. Rewording: Repeating information provided by sources to clarify and validate their understanding.

Reformulation, like a magnifying glass scrutinizing the smallest details, is an essential skill in the field of intelligence. This technique consists of repeating and summarizing the information provided by the sources to ensure mutual understanding and accurate validation of the data collected.

In the intelligence context, reformulation plays a crucial role in interviews, interrogations and exchanges with sources. The aim is to clarify the information gathered, avoid misunderstandings and obtain further clarification if necessary. By reformulating the information, the intelligence professional shows the source that he is attentive to his words, while giving him the opportunity to confirm or correct his statements.

The reformulation is also part of a process of validation of the information. By repeating the details provided by the source, the intelligence professional can detect any inconsistencies or contradictions. This allows him to ensure that the information is reliable and that it corresponds to the real facts.

It is important to stress that the reformulation must be carried out with tact and diplomacy. It's not about putting the source on the defensive or making it feel judged. On the contrary, it is essential to create a climate of trust and respect, showing at the source that its contribution is valuable and taken seriously.

Rewording can be used in different ways depending on the context of the interaction. For example, during an interrogation, the intelligence professional may rephrase the source's responses to ensure consistency in their account. During an interview, he can repeat the words of the source to show that he is listening and to encourage it to deepen its explanations.

In addition to ensuring a better understanding and validation of information, the reformulation also strengthens the link between the intelligence professional and the source. It shows that the professional is truly involved in the conversation and that he values the words of the source.

45. Open questioning: Ask open-ended questions to encourage sources to express themselves freely.

Open questioning, as a lever to open the doors of dialogue, is a fundamental technique for any intelligence professional. This approach involves asking questions that do not require short or limited answers, but instead encourage sources to express themselves in a detailed and free way.

In the intelligence context, open questioning is particularly valuable during interviews and interrogations with sources. Rather than soliciting factual or limited answers, the intelligence professional chooses questions that encourage sources to share their knowledge, experiences, and opinions in depth.

One of the main strengths of open questioning is its ability to provide rich and nuanced information. By giving sources the opportunity to express themselves freely, the intelligence professional can gather detailed data and varied perspectives on a given topic. This provides a more complete and accurate picture of the situation under study.

In addition, open questioning fosters the establishment of a climate of trust and cooperation between the intelligence professional and the source. By showing a genuine interest in what the source has to say and by offering it a space to express itself, the professional shows his respect and consideration for it. This may encourage the source to feel comfortable sharing sensitive or confidential information.

In addition, open questioning can also serve as a trigger to explore unexpected or unanticipated aspects of a situation. By encouraging sources to speak freely, the intelligence professional can uncover relevant details or unpublished information that might have gone unnoticed with more closed-ended questions.

However, it is essential to master the art of open questioning to take full advantage of it. Questions should be formulated in a clear and precise manner, without inducing or influencing the answers of the source. The professional must also be active listening and patient, avoiding interrupting the source when it is spoken.

46. Use of negotiation techniques: Finding compromises to obtain information from reluctant sources.

The art of negotiation proves to be an invaluable asset in obtaining crucial information from reluctant sources. This subtle and strategic technique involves finding skillful and balanced compromises that meet the needs of the intelligence professional while respecting the interests and concerns of the source.

When faced with sources that may be suspicious, fearful or hesitant to disclose sensitive information, the intelligence professional must demonstrate a patient and diplomatic approach. Negotiation is not about forcing or manipulating the source, but rather about establishing a constructive dialogue where both parties can agree on acceptable terms.

The first step in negotiation is to listen carefully to the concerns and objections of the source. Understanding the motivations and fears behind one's reluctance is essential to finding appropriate solutions. By showing empathy and interest in the needs of the source, the intelligence professional can create a climate of trust conducive to negotiation.

Then, it is a question of finding creative and equitable solutions that both obtain the information sought and meet the needs of the source. This may involve offering incentives or benefits that motivate the source to cooperate. For example, offering protection or assistance in exchange for sensitive information can be an effective incentive for some sources.

However, it is important to ensure that trade-offs do not compromise the integrity of the investigation or intelligence operations. The line between legitimate negotiation and compromise of ethical principles can be fine. The intelligence professional should always keep in mind that the collection of information must be conducted in a manner that is lawful, ethical, and respectful of individual rights.

On the other hand, negotiation can also be used to gain the trust and cooperation of potential sources even before they become reluctant. By taking a persuasive and caring approach, the intelligence professional can build trusting relationships from the beginning, which in turn facilitates the collection of information.

47. Emotion management: Control your own emotions to maintain professional behavior.

When interacting with sources, intelligence professionals may be confronted with stressful, sensitive, or emotionally charged situations. In such circumstances, it is crucial to keep your cool and not let your emotions take over. Managing emotions involves recognizing and understanding one's own feelings while preventing them from negatively affecting the information-gathering process.

A first step in managing emotions is becoming aware of them. The intelligence professional must be able to identify their emotions and understand what triggers them. This helps prevent impulsive or inappropriate reactions that could affect the quality of interaction with the source.

Controlling your emotions also involves the ability to stay calm and focused even in tense situations. Stress and pressure can be commonplace in intelligence, and it is essential to develop stress management techniques to deal with these situations without compromising the quality of work.

Effective communication with sources also requires knowing how to express emotions appropriately. It is important to communicate clearly and respectfully, avoiding emotional or impulsive reactions that could alter the relationship of trust with the source.

Finally, managing emotions also involves knowing when to step back and temporarily withdraw from a situation if necessary. If emotions become too intense or the situation becomes too difficult to manage, it is important to know how to withdraw to avoid any harm to the collection of information.

48. Using validation: Recognizing the feelings and opinions of others to build trust.

The use of validation is a powerful technique in the field of intelligence, as it builds trust between the professional and the source. Validation is about recognizing the feelings, opinions, and experiences of the source in an empathetic and respectful way.

When interacting with sources, it is essential to show empathy and understanding towards their feelings and points of view. This allows the source to feel listened to and understood, which strengthens the bond of trust and encourages the source to be more open and cooperative.

Validation can take different forms, such as listening attentively to the emotions expressed by the source, acknowledging the legitimacy of one's opinions even if they differ from one's own, and expressing understanding of one's lived experiences. For example, saying something like "I understand this must have been a difficult situation for you" or "I see you're passionate about this issue" shows the source that their feelings and opinions are taken into account and respected.

By using validation, the intelligence professional demonstrates a commitment to treating the source with respect and consideration. This helps create an environment of trust in which the source feels safe to share sensitive and confidential information.

Validation is also an effective tool for defusing situations of conflict or tension. When the source expresses strong emotions or divergent opinions, validation calms spirits and promotes constructive dialogue. By acknowledging the feelings of the source, the intelligence professional shows that he is open to hearing his point of view and is willing to work together to find solutions.

However, it is important to note that validation must be used with authenticity and sincerity. The sources are often very intuitive and can quickly detect if the validation is feigned or manipulative. It is therefore crucial to show genuine empathy and interest in the feelings and opinions of the source.

In conclusion, the use of validation is an essential technique to build trust between the intelligence professional and the source. By showing empathy and acknowledging the feelings and opinions of the source, the professional creates an environment of trust conducive to the collection of sensitive and relevant information. Validation is a powerful tool to defuse tensions and foster constructive dialogue, while maintaining respectful and professional behaviour.

49. Use of positive body language: Adopt an open posture and friendly gestures to encourage positive communication.

The use of positive body language is an essential skill for intelligence professionals when interacting with sources. Body language includes gestures, facial expressions, posture, and other nonverbal cues that can communicate powerful messages, sometimes even more than the words themselves. Adopting positive body language is an effective strategy to encourage positive communication and build trust with the source.

When an intelligence professional adopts an open posture, with uncrossed arms and a slight forward tilt, he shows the source that he is attentive and receptive to what it has to say. It also indicates that the professional is open to communication and ready to actively listen to the source.

Similarly, using friendly and warm gestures can help create an environment conducive to positive communication. Gestures such as smiling, nodding to show approval, or using encouraging signals, such as a thumbs up, can build trust and encourage the source to continue sharing information.

It is also important to show respect for the source by avoiding actions that could be perceived as hostile or selfless. For example, avoiding folding your arms can be interpreted as a sign of closure or disagreement. Similarly, avoiding looking at your watch or appearing distracted can give the impression that the professional does not attach importance to the information provided by the source.

Another important aspect of positive body language is adapting to the culture and social norms of the source. Some gestures or postures can have a different meaning depending on the culture, and it is essential to take them into account to avoid any misunderstanding or misunderstanding.

In summary, the use of positive body language is a powerful way for intelligence professionals to create an environment of positive communication and build trust with the source. By adopting an open posture, using friendly gestures and showing respect for the source, the professional creates a climate conducive to the collection of valuable information and the establishment of a lasting relationship of trust. Positive body language is a valuable tool that effectively complements the verbal skills of the intelligence professional and contributes to the success of his mission.

50. Flexibility: Adapt to different communication styles of customers and sources.

Flexibility is an essential skill for intelligence professionals, as they often interact with clients and sources with varying communication styles. Being able to adapt to these different styles of communication is fundamental to establishing a relationship of trust and obtaining valuable information.

Each individual has their own way of communicating, which can be influenced by factors such as culture, personality, context and life experience. Some clients or sources may be direct and assertive, while others may be more reserved and prefer a softer approach. As an intelligence professional, it is important to recognize these differences and adapt accordingly.

The first step to being flexible in communication is to observe and listen carefully to the person in front of you. By observing his body language, tone of voice and facial expressions, one can get indications of his preferred communication style. By actively listening to what she is saying and asking open-ended questions, we can also better understand her needs and expectations.

Then, it is essential to adjust your own communication style according to that of the person in front of you. If the source prefers a direct and concise approach, it is best to be clear and concise in their questions and answers. If the source seems more comfortable with a more informal and warm approach, it is possible to adopt a friendly tone and create a friendly environment.

Flexibility in communication also involves showing empathy and understanding towards the person in front of you. It means recognizing and respecting your emotions, opinions, and needs, even if they differ from your own. By showing empathy, the intelligence professional creates a climate of trust and shows the person that he or she is heard and taken into account.

Finally, it is important to keep in mind that flexibility in communication does not mean giving up one's own principles or values. Rather, it is about finding a balance between adapting to the needs of the person in front of you while maintaining their integrity and professionalism.

In conclusion, flexibility in communication is a crucial skill for intelligence professionals. Being able to adapt to the different communication styles of clients and sources helps to build trust, gain valuable information, and successfully complete intelligence assignments. By observing, listening, adjusting style, and showing empathy, the intelligence professional can be effective and professional in their interactions with others. Flexibility in communication is a valuable asset that contributes to the success of intelligence missions and the development of lasting relationships of trust.

51. Use of hypothetical scenarios: Ask questions about fictional scenarios to get more honest answers.

Using what-if scenarios is an effective technique for intelligence professionals when they want more honest and candid answers from their sources. This approach circumvents certain psychological and social barriers that can limit the disclosure of sensitive or compromising information.

When sources are confronted with direct questions about their actual activities or intentions, they may be inclined to be reluctant or provide answers that conceal the truth. This may be due to fear of retaliation, embarrassment, or simply the desire to protect their privacy.

Using what-if scenarios, intelligence professionals can create a secure and non-threatening environment for their sources. They may ask about fictional situations or hypothetical scenarios that are similar to real-life situations, but allow the source to express itself without directly revealing sensitive information.

For example, instead of asking a source directly if they have had any interactions with a specific organization, the intelligence professional might ask a hypothetical question like, "What would you do if you were contacted by that organization?" This gives the source the opportunity to talk about their potential reactions without feeling compelled to disclose confidential information.

Hypothetical scenarios can also be used to probe the motivations and intentions of sources. For example, instead of asking a source directly why they got involved in a certain activity, the intelligence professional might ask a question like, "Let's say you decided to get involved in that activity. What would have prompted you to do it?" This provides information about factors that could influence the source without putting it in an awkward position.

When using hypothetical scenarios, it is important that the intelligence professional clearly explain to the source that the situations presented are fictitious and that the answers provided will be treated with the same confidentiality as any other information. This helps build trust and encourage the source to be honest in their answers.

52. Clear objective setting: Clearly communicate survey objectives to clients and sources.

Setting clear objectives is a crucial step in any investigative process, whether it is intelligence or any other information-gathering activity. This technique involves accurately and transparently communicating the objectives of the survey to clients and sources, to ensure a mutual understanding of expectations and expected outcomes.

For clients, it is essential to understand the reasons and motivations behind the investigation. By clearly communicating objectives, intelligence professionals help clients define their specific information needs and formulate relevant questions. This step also ensures that the investigation is aligned with the client's priorities and values, and that it respects ethical and legal boundaries.

When it comes to communicating objectives to sources, transparency is equally important. Sources need to understand why they are being solicited and what information is being sought. By clearly explaining the objectives of the investigation, intelligence professionals build trust with sources, which facilitates cooperation and disclosure of relevant information.

To effectively communicate the objectives of the investigation, intelligence professionals must use clear and unambiguous language. They should avoid technical terms or jargon that might be misunderstood by customers and sources. By using simple and accessible language, they ensure that everyone is on the same page and that the goals are well understood.

In addition, it is essential to listen carefully to clients and sources to ensure that their needs are well understood and that objectives are adapted accordingly. If necessary, intelligence professionals should clarify expectations and adjust objectives to meet the specific needs of each party.

Finally, it is important to document the objectives of the investigation and share them with all parties involved. This allows for a clear and formal reference of the agreed objectives, which avoids any confusion or discrepancies later on.

53. Assertive communication: Expressing opinions and needs in a direct and respectful manner.

Assertive communication is an essential skill for intelligence professionals. It is about expressing opinions, needs and ideas in a direct, clear and respectful way, while taking into account the rights and opinions of others.

In the context of intelligence, assertive communication is particularly important when interacting with sources and clients. It allows intelligence professionals to effectively convey the necessary information, ask relevant questions and clearly articulate the objectives of the investigation.

One of the key characteristics of assertive communication is to be direct and frank in your words, without being aggressive or offensive. It means expressing one's thoughts and opinions in a respectful manner, without minimizing or ignoring the rights and views of others.

For example, when interviewing a source, an intelligence professional may use assertive communication to ask direct and specific questions on sensitive topics, while ensuring that the dignity and confidentiality of the source is respected.

Similarly, when presenting the results of a survey to a client, assertive communication helps to provide clear and concise information, while being open to comments and questions from the client.

Another important facet of assertive communication is the ability to actively listen to others and consider their views. It means being open to different opinions and ideas, and being willing to question your own beliefs if necessary.

Assertive communication also allows you to resolve conflicts constructively and defend your rights and interests without being aggressive or passive. It fosters positive and respectful professional relationships, which helps to build trust and cooperation between the various parties involved in the intelligence process.

In conclusion, assertive communication is an essential skill for intelligence professionals. It allows people to express their opinions, needs and ideas in a direct and respectful manner, while taking into account the rights and opinions of others. This approach promotes positive and constructive interactions with sources and clients, which contributes to successful investigations and relevant and reliable information.

54. Use of humor: Use humor to relax the atmosphere and facilitate communication.

The use of humor is a subtle but powerful technique for intelligence professionals. In situations where sensitive information is gathered, the atmosphere can sometimes be tense and the topics discussed can be tricky. Well-balanced humor can be an effective way to lighten the mood and connect with sources or customers.

When used appropriately, humour can help break the ice and build trust. A well-placed joke can help defuse tension and make the interaction more enjoyable and relaxed. It can also help reduce the stress and anxiety that sources may feel when communicating sensitive information.

However, it is important to exercise caution and discernment in the use of humor. Not all situations lend themselves to humor, and some people may have particular sensitivities. It is therefore essential to know your audience and make sure that the humor is appropriate in the given context.

In addition, it is important to never use humor to minimize or ridicule serious topics or important information. Humour must be used with respect and tact, without ever compromising the integrity of the investigation or the relationship with sources and clients.

55. Anticipating objections: Anticipating potential objections and responding proactively.

Anticipating objections is an essential skill for intelligence professionals when interacting with sources or clients. This technique involves anticipating potential objections that interlocutors might raise and responding to them proactively, even before they are expressed.

By anticipating objections, intelligence professionals can prepare to provide clear and convincing answers. This helps to strengthen the credibility of the investigation and show sources and clients that they are knowledgeable and ready to deal with any questions or concerns.

There are different ways to anticipate objections. First, it is important to know the context of the investigation and sensitive topics that could elicit negative reactions. By identifying potential sticking points, intelligence professionals can prepare to proactively address them.

Then, it helps to put yourself in the other person's shoes and consider any concerns they may have. By having an empathetic understanding of the perspectives and interests of the interlocutors, intelligence professionals can better anticipate objections and respond appropriately.

Another approach is to consult colleagues or experts in the field to get different opinions and broaden the perspective. This can help identify alternative points of view or issues that one would not have thought of.

When interacting with sources or clients, intelligence professionals can use assertive communication techniques to anticipate objections. For example, they can introduce the survey by highlighting the positive aspects or potential benefits for the interlocutors. This can help prevent objections related to the usefulness or relevance of the survey.

Finally, it is important to be open and responsive to interlocutors' questions and concerns. If objections are raised, it is essential to respond respectfully and provide additional information if necessary.

56. Use of emotional argument: Using moving stories to elicit empathy and interest.

The use of emotional argument is a powerful technique for intelligence professionals. By telling moving stories, they seek to elicit empathy and interest in their interlocutors, whether they are sources or customers.

Moving stories have the power to touch people's deepest emotions and values. They make it possible to create an emotional connection with the interlocutors by involving them personally in the story. This can help make them more receptive to the information and objectives of the survey.

To use the emotional argument effectively, it is essential to choose stories that are relevant and authentic. These stories should be relevant to the subject of the investigation and reflect real-life situations that have an emotional impact.

For example, when an intelligence professional seeks to convince a source to disclose sensitive information, he or she may share a poignant story about the positive consequences such disclosure could have for public safety or the protection of human rights. This approach can affect the sensitivity of the source and push it to cooperate.

Similarly, when an intelligence professional presents the results of an investigation to a client, the use of a moving story can help illustrate the importance and relevance of the information gathered. It can also lead to stronger client engagement with the survey and recommended actions.

However, it is essential to use the emotional argument carefully and ethically. Moving stories should never be manipulative or false. It is important to ensure that the information shared is accurate and relevant, and not to exploit the emotions of the interlocutors for malicious purposes.

57. Using the step-by-step approach: Break complex problems into steps that are easier to solve.

The technique of breaking complex problems into easier-to-solve steps is an essential tool used by intelligence professionals to approach investigations and missions in a methodical and organized manner. This approach simplifies seemingly insurmountable tasks by breaking them down into manageable steps, making them easier to resolve efficiently.

The first step in this technique is to understand the problem as a whole and identify the different parts that compose it. This may involve gathering relevant information, analysing available data and consulting experts in the relevant field.

Once the problem has been clearly defined, the second step is to break it down into more specific and manageable sub-problems. Each sub-issue can be addressed individually, allowing for more focused efforts and resources.

The third step is to establish an action plan to solve each sub-problem. This involves determining the resources needed, setting specific objectives and defining the steps to be taken to achieve these objectives.

Once the action plans are in place, the fourth step is to implement the strategies defined for each sub-issue. This step often involves collaboration with other members of the intelligence team, the use of different investigative methods and techniques, and the collection and analysis of additional data.

The fifth step is evaluation and review. Once each sub-issue has been resolved, it is essential to reassess the entire issue to ensure that all parties have been considered and that the overall objectives have been met.

Finally, the final step is to learn from the whole process. This involves reflecting on challenges, successes and lessons learned. These lessons can be used to improve the methods and approaches used in future surveys.

58. Values-based persuasion: Find arguments that align with the values and interests of the sources.

Values-based persuasion is an essential communication technique used by intelligence professionals to convince sources to cooperate and disclose sensitive information. This approach involves identifying the values and interests of the sources, and then tailoring the persuasive arguments based on these elements.

The first step in this technique is to understand the values and interests of the source. This can be accomplished by asking open-ended questions and listening carefully to the answers provided by the source. It is important to create an environment of trust and respect to encourage the source to open up and express its beliefs.

Once the values and interests of the source have been identified, the second step is to formulate the persuasive arguments with an emphasis on these elements. For example, if the source places a high value on public safety, the intelligence professional may highlight how the cooperation of the source can help protect society and prevent threats.

The third step is to link the source values to the objectives of the survey. This involves demonstrating how the cooperation of the source can help achieve goals that are aligned with one's personal values. For example, if the source is concerned about environmental protection, the intelligence professional can show how the information provided can help combat activities that are harmful to the environment.

Finally, the fourth step is to present the arguments for persuasion in a clear and convincing manner. This may involve the use of solid evidence, credible testimonies and concrete examples to illustrate the benefits of cooperation from the source. It is also important to respond to the source's questions and concerns in an honest and transparent manner.

59. Use of social influence: Highlight the actions or opinions of others to encourage cooperation.

The use of social influence is an effective persuasion technique used by intelligence professionals to encourage the cooperation of sources. This approach is based on the premise that individuals are often influenced by the actions and opinions of others, and that highlighting examples of cooperation or commitment from others can encourage a source to follow their example.

The first step in this technique is to identify relevant examples of social influence. This may involve highlighting cases where other sources have cooperated and benefited from this collaboration. It is important to choose examples that are consistent with the values and interests of the source, so that they can identify with these other people.

Once examples of social influence have been identified, the second step is to present them at the source in a persuasive manner. This can be accomplished by highlighting the benefits and advantages that others have experienced by cooperating, as well as the positive results that have resulted from their collaboration. It is also useful to highlight the satisfaction and recognition these individuals have received for contributing to successful intelligence efforts.

The third step is to encourage the source to consider how it could benefit from the cooperation itself. This may involve asking open-ended questions and prompting reflections on the potential benefits of cooperation, both personally and professionally. It is important to create an environment of trust and respect so that the source feels comfortable sharing their thoughts and considerations.

Finally, the fourth step is to maintain open communication with the source and offer ongoing support throughout the cooperation process. It is essential to answer her questions, resolve her concerns and support her in her efforts to contribute to intelligence objectives.

In conclusion, the use of social influence is a powerful persuasion technique used by intelligence professionals to encourage the cooperation of sources. Highlighting examples of others who have successfully cooperated and highlighting the benefits of collaboration can positively influence the source's decision to engage in the intelligence process. However, it is essential to use this technique ethically, respecting the rights and dignity of sources, and ensuring that their cooperation is voluntary and informed.

60. Use of the "foot in the door" technique: Ask for a small favor first and then get more cooperation.

The "foot in the door" technique is a subtle but effective persuasion strategy used by intelligence professionals to enlist the cooperation of sources. This approach is based on the psychological principle that individuals are more inclined to accept larger and larger requests once they have already accepted a smaller request.

The first step in this technique is to formulate an initial request that is relatively small and easy for the source to accept. This can be something simple, such as answering a few questions or providing basic information. The goal is to get an initial commitment from the source, even if it's a small step towards cooperation.

Once the source has accepted the initial request, the second step is to formulate a larger and more demanding request. This may be a request for deeper cooperation, to provide more sensitive information, or to engage in closer collaboration with intelligence professionals. By using the "foot in the door" technique, the chances that the source will accept this greater request are greatly increased, because it already feels engaged in the process of cooperation.

The third step is to continue to nurture the relationship with the source and support it throughout the cooperation process. It is essential to maintain open communication and answer questions and concerns honestly and transparently.

Finally, the fourth step is to recognize and appreciate the cooperation of the source. It is important to show gratitude and recognize the value of the information provided by the source. This strengthens the relationship of trust and encourages the source to continue to cooperate in the future.

61. Use of the "door to the nose" technique: First ask for a big favor that you know is denied and then ask for a more reasonable favor.

The "door to nose" technique is a subtle persuasion approach used by intelligence professionals to obtain the cooperation of sources. This strategy is based on the psychological principle that individuals are more likely to accept a more reasonable request after refusing a larger and unreasonable request.

The first step in this technique is to formulate an initial request that is deliberately large and difficult for the source to accept. The objective is to provoke a refusal, which is expected and expected by the intelligence professional. This initial request can be something demanding, such as providing highly sensitive information or engaging in very intensive cooperation.

Once the source has denied the initial request, the second step is to make a second, more reasonable and acceptable request. This request is designed to be perceived as a concession on the part of the intelligence professional, after having made such a demanding previous request. The source is more likely to feel inclined to accept this more reasonable request, as they will feel indebted to the intelligence professional for making a concession.

The third step is to continue to nurture the relationship with the source and support it throughout the cooperation process. It is essential to maintain open communication and answer your questions and concerns honestly and transparently. The intelligence professional must demonstrate that he values the cooperation of the source and that he recognizes the value of the information provided.

62. Use of the "priming" technique: Present advance information that influences subsequent responses.

The "priming" technique is a persuasion strategy used by intelligence professionals to influence a source's subsequent responses by presenting it with advance information. This approach is based on the psychological principle that individuals are influenced by the information they are exposed to first, and this can affect their perceptions and decisions later.

The first step in this technique is to present advance information to the source, often in the form of a question or statement. This information is chosen in such a way as to influence the thoughts or emotions of the source in a specific way. For example, by asking a question that assumes a positive answer, the intelligence professional can influence the source to give more favourable answers later.

Once the primer has been completed, the second step is to ask questions or formulate requests that are in line with the advance information. The source is then more likely to respond consistently with the initial priming, as this unconsciously influences the way it thinks and perceives things.

It is important to note that the use of the priming technique must be carried out ethically and responsibly. The goal is not to manipulate or deceive the source, but rather to elicit more informative responses using prior information that is relevant to the ongoing investigation.

63. Use of the "trap" technique: Ask obvious questions that the source is tempted to answer falsely to test their sincerity.

The "trap" technique is a subtle method of testing the sincerity of sources by asking them obvious questions that they are tempted to answer falsely. This approach aims to assess the honesty and credibility of the source by observing its reaction to ambiguous or sensitive situations.

The first step in this technique is to formulate questions that are easily verifiable or to which the source should know the answers, either because they are public knowledge or because they directly concern their own area of expertise. However, these questions are worded in such a way that the answers are not obvious, and the source is tempted to lie to give himself an appearance of knowledge or to hide certain information.

The second step is to carefully observe the answers from the source. If the source answers honestly and accurately, it can be a sign of sincerity and credibility. On the other hand, if the source provides evasive, contradictory or false answers, it can be an indicator of lack of confidence in the veracity of his words.

It is important to note that the use of the "trap" technique should be carried out with caution and discernment. The goal is not to trap or deceive the source, but rather to test its sincerity and credibility in the ongoing investigation.

In conclusion, the "trap" technique is a verification approach used by intelligence professionals to test the sincerity and credibility of sources. By asking obvious questions that the source is tempted to answer falsely, intelligence professionals can assess the honesty of the source and the reliability of the information provided. However, it is essential to remember that manipulation or coercion of sources is not acceptable, and that the use of this technique must be guided by ethical principles and high professional standards.

64. Use of the "lie by omission" technique: Omitting important information to influence the responses or decisions of sources.

This approach aims to guide the perception of the source by providing only partial or biased information, which may lead it to make decisions or provide information that is consistent with the intelligence professional's objectives.

The first step in this technique is to identify important information that could influence the source's responses or decisions. This information can be key facts, events, or details that could alter the source's perspective on the situation in question.

The second step is to deliberately omit this information when interacting with the source. This can be done by avoiding asking specific questions or deftly diverting attention from certain information.

The third step is to carefully observe the reaction of the source and the information it provides. If the source reacts in a manner consistent with the intelligence professional's expectations, this may indicate that the "lie by omission" has succeeded in influencing their responses or decisions.

65. Use of the "signposting" technique: Drawing the source's attention to a specific point to divert their attention from other aspects.

The "signposting" technique is a manipulation strategy used by intelligence professionals to draw the source's attention to a specific point, in order to divert their attention from other important aspects. This approach aims to orient the perception of the source by focusing on a particular piece of information or topic, while avoiding mentioning sensitive details or issues.

The first step in this technique is to identify the information or topics that the intelligence professional wishes to divert from the source's attention. This information can be critical elements or sensitive questions that could influence the answers or decisions of the source.

The second step is to subtly direct the conversation to the specific point the intelligence professional wants to highlight. This can be done by asking specific questions, using anecdotes or examples that highlight the target point.

The third step is to keep the source's attention on the specific point throughout the interaction. This can be done by regularly returning to the topic, asking related questions that reinforce the highlighted point, or using gestures and facial expressions to grab the source's attention.

The main purpose of "signposting" is to maintain control of the conversation and divert attention from the source of sensitive information or issues. This can allow the intelligence professional to manipulate the perception of the source and obtain answers or information that are consistent with their objectives.

In conclusion, the technique of "signposting" is a manipulation strategy used by intelligence professionals to draw the attention of the source to a specific point, in order to divert their attention from other important aspects. While this approach may be effective in some cases, it raises important ethical questions and should be used with caution and discernment. Intelligence professionals must always act ethically and transparently, avoiding manipulation or deception of sources.

66. Use of the "urgency" technique: Create a sense of urgency to prompt sources to act quickly.

The "emergency" technique is a manipulative approach used by intelligence professionals to create a sense of urgency in sources, thereby prompting them to act quickly and often impulsively. This strategy aims to harness the natural human response to urgent situations, which can lead individuals to make hasty decisions without having time to think critically.

The first step in this technique is to create a situation or context that gives the impression that urgent action is needed. This can be done by presenting an imminent threat, an opportunity that will only last for a very short time, or by pointing out the negative consequences of not acting quickly.

The second step is to increase the urgency and put pressure on the source to make a quick decision. This can be done by using phrases like "there is no time to lose", "it is now or never", or by emphasizing the negative consequences of not acting immediately.

The third step is to narrow the source's options and direct it to the desired action. This can be done by limiting the information available, presenting a single option as the best solution, or using persuasive tactics to encourage the source to act in accordance with the intelligence professional's objectives.

The main goal of the "emergency" technique is to push the source to make impulsive decisions and act quickly, without having time to think critically or evaluate all available options. This allows the intelligence professional to manipulate the source's reaction and push it to act in accordance with its own interests.

Conclusion

The book we went through together is a comprehensive resource on offensive intelligence, aimed at anyone interested in the art of gathering information for various missions. With a didactic and pedagogical approach, it provides essential tools for private investigators, police officers, business intelligence consultants, as well as for citizens wishing to understand and master intelligence techniques.

The first part of the book deals with HUMINT, one of the key approaches to intelligence. HUMINT is based on human interaction and gathering information directly from sources. We explored the different techniques of direct interviewing, testimonial collection, informant recruitment, neighborhood investigation, use of decoys, and much more. Each technique is presented in a concrete way, with examples and practical tips to implement them successfully.

In the second part of the book, we explored OSINT, another crucial facet of offensive intelligence. OSINT focuses on gathering information from publicly available sources. We discovered how to leverage conventional search engines, use Boolean operators to refine results, explore public databases, and much more. This section highlights the wealth of information available online and highlights the importance of OSINT in intelligence operations.

The third part of the book focused on source manipulation techniques, an essential aspect of offensive intelligence. These techniques allow intelligence professionals to influence sources and gather information effectively. We explored strategies such as using empathy, rewording, using humor, managing emotions, and many more. This section emphasizes the importance of effective communication and building trusting relationships with sources.

In summary, this book offers a comprehensive and detailed exploration of offensive intelligence, with a particular focus on HUMINT, OSINT, and source manipulation techniques. Each chapter offers practical tips, concrete examples and proven strategies to improve information gathering and analytical skills. It invites readers to develop an ethical and responsible approach to intelligence, emphasizing respect for individual rights and privacy.

Throughout this book, the mysterious author has shared his expertise and knowledge, while keeping his identity a secret. Whether he is a former agent of a domestic intelligence service, an intelligence advisor to an African head of state, or an expert in economic intelligence, the bottom line is that his teachings enrich our understanding of offensive intelligence.

Nevertheless, it is essential to emphasize that intelligence must be used responsibly and ethically. Readers should always respect laws, rules, and individual rights when collecting and using information. The author declines all responsibility for any malicious use of the techniques presented in this book. Intelligence must always be exercised in accordance with law and ethics, taking care to protect the rights and dignity of individuals.

In conclusion, this book paves the way for a better understanding of offensive intelligence and offers valuable skills for private investigators, police officers, business intelligence consultants, and ordinary citizens eager to engage in the world of information gathering. By using the techniques presented in this book in an ethical and responsible manner, readers will be able to strengthen their intelligence skills and contribute to more informed and safe decision-making.

Printed in Poland
by Amazon Fulfillment
Poland Sp. z o.o., Wrocław